GREGORIAN CHANT

GREGORIAN CHANT

A Guide to the History and Liturgy

DOM DANIEL SAULNIER, OSB
PROFESSOR OF GREGORIAN CHANT
PONTIFICAL INSTITUTE OF SACRED MUSIC IN ROME

TRANSLATED BY DR. MARY BERRY, CBE
FOUNDER AND DIRECTOR OF THE SCHOLA GREGORIANA, CAMBRIDGE

VISUAL & PERFORMING ARTS

PARACLETE PRESS
BREWSTER, MASSACHUSETTS

Gregorian Chant: A Guide to the History and Liturgy

2009 First Printing This Translation in English
2003 First Printing This Edition in French

Copyright © 2003, S.A. La Froidfontaine, France

ISBN 978-1-55725-554-9

This book was first published in 1995 thanks to the *Centre Culturel de l'Ouest et de la région des Pays de la Loire*. The present edition offers a number of corrections.

Library of Congress Cataloging-in-Publication Data

Saulnier, Daniel.
    [Chant grégorien. English]
    Gregorian chant : a guide to the history and liturgy / Daniel Saulnier ; translated by Mary Berry.
        p. cm.
    Includes bibliographical references.
    ISBN 978-1-55725-554-9
    1. Gregorian chants--History and criticism. I. Title.
    ML3082.S2713 2009
    782.32'22--dc22
                                        2009003951

10 9 8 7 6 5 4 3 2 1

Published by Paraclete Press
Brewster, Massachusetts
www.paracletepress.com

Printed in the United States of America using paper with 30% post-consumer waste. Trees were responsibly harvested following sustainable forestry guidelines. No trees from ancient forests were used in the making of the paper.

In memory of Canon Jean Jeanneteau

CONTENTS

A NOTE FROM THE PUBLISHER
ABOUT THIS EDITION

At the request of Paraclete Press, Dr. Mary Berry, CBE, founder of the Schola Gregoriana in Cambridge, England, translated this book into English. The French edition was written by Dom Daniel Saulnier, OSB, and entitled *Le Chant grégorien par un moine de Solesmes.*

By the time of her death in 2008, Dr. Berry had completed her work and approved minor changes. It fell to the editorial staff at Paraclete Press to assemble the various chapters in the spirit of the French original and the translator's style. Since this work was completed posthumously, any errors in the text are the responsibility of the publisher and not of Dr. Mary Berry, a renowned and accomplished scholar, and an inspired friend.

1

HISTORY

*I am searching everywhere to find out about
what people thought, what they did, and what they
loved in the Church throughout the
ages of faith.*

DOM GUÉRANGER

About two thousand years ago, the Christian message
left the holy city of Jerusalem and the lands of Syria
and Palestine and spread rapidly all around the basin of
the Mediterranean. As the message spread, so also the
practice of Christian worship—what we know as the
liturgy, or public prayer—was being developed. Since this
was a time when any idea of centralization was completely
unknown, each region was soon celebrating the liturgy,
and therefore singing it, in its own language.

This diversity of language has been maintained up to the
present day in the liturgies of the Middle East. In the lands of
the western Mediterranean, it would be different. After the
first two centuries when the liturgy was celebrated in Greek,
Latin—the language of everyday life—came to be used more
and more. So each region of the Christian West began to
have a repertory of sacred music of its own: there was a

single language but different texts and music. We know for certain that there existed:

- Beneventan chant, in southern Italy,

- Roman chant, in the city of Rome and its dependencies,

- Milanese chant, in northern Italy,

- Hispanic chant, on both sides of the Pyrenees,

- One, or perhaps several types of Gallican chant, in the lands of Roman Gaul.

ROMAN ORIGINS

Of all these different repertories of Latin chant in early Western Europe, the Milanese is the only one to be still in use today. The church of Milan has indeed preserved its own liturgy, not without some difficulty or compromise. The chant is still called "Ambrosian," from the name of the spiritual protector of this whole tradition, the Bishop St. Ambrose (d. 397). It is to be found in manuscripts of the twelfth century.

As for the ancient Roman tradition, we learn about it from certain rather vague historical references,[1] but especially from the Sacramentaries.[2] So we are well informed about the ordering of the ancient Roman liturgy,[3] but what about the chant? It could certainly have come to us only through oral transmission. Five books, dating from between the eleventh and the thirteenth centuries, have brought us the repertory as it was sung in certain of the Roman basilicas of that period. Even if there was any distortion or corruption, this must have been minimal, for there are few variant readings among the five manuscripts. These sources make it possible for us to recapture to a large extent the tradition of the Old Roman chant.[4]

In essence, the composition of the Roman repertory dates from the fifth to sixth centuries. The Church had been free of persecutions since the beginning of the fourth century; even the administrative structure of the Roman Empire seems to have, as it were, passed into its hands. The building of the great basilicas had made it possible for public worship to take a great leap forward and to assume a new dignity. All the arts were making their contribution, and music had its place as well. It is a fact that up to that time most of the singing had been the preserve of the solo cantor. But the *schola cantorum* made its appearance at this moment, a group of about twenty clergy (experienced cantors and young pupils in training) who would place their competence at the service of liturgical celebration. Between the sixth and seventh centuries, this specialized group developed a repertory of sacred music made up of two categories of pieces.

The first category was a revision of the existing repertory. From then on, the *schola* was to replace the solo cantor for the performance of certain pieces, which up to that time would have been reserved for him, but would now be given by them a more elaborate style and a structure of greater complexity.

The second was the composition of fresh chants, linked to the development of spacious basilicas and to the ceremonial they command; one example of this would have been the chant called for by an imposing procession during the solemn entry of the celebrant.

By the time of Pope Gregory I (590), the composition of the whole corpus of Roman melodies would appear to have been completed.

THE FRANKISH-ROMAN MERGING

During the second half of the eighth century, a rapprochement was beginning to take place between the Frankish kingdom (of Pépin the Short and his son Charlemagne), and the papacy (Stephen II and his successors). This rapprochement was at first political: the estates of the papacy were being threatened by the Lombards, whereas the young king of the Franks was anxious to ensure the legitimacy of his right to a throne conquered after a severe struggle. Pépin the Short promised to protect the papal estates, and the pope came to France with his court, renewed the consecration of the king of the Franks, and made a long stay at the Abbey of Saint-Denis.

These events led to the new ruler's appreciation of Roman liturgical customs. Pépin the Short realized that these customs could help to ensure religious unity through-out his territories and thus strengthen their political unity. He therefore commanded that the Roman liturgy be adopted throughout his kingdom.

The introduction of the Roman liturgy had the practical result of suppressing the Gallican chant repertory and replacing it with the Roman. We can find, too, in the correspondence and chronicles of the time, several mentions of requests in Gaul for books from Rome. Books were sent and there were exchanges of cantors, because no musical notation for the chant was in existence at that period; the best that could be done was to send books containing the words, minus their melodies.

No written account has come down to us of what happened at that moment, in the second half of the eighth century, in Frankish Gaul between the Seine and the Rhine. Could the changeover perhaps have taken place at Metz? Liturgists and musicologists have compared the eleventh- to thirteenth-century Roman service-books with the Gregorian ones. Their conclusions lead to the following hypothesis, which seems highly probable:[5] at the time of the encounter between the two repertories, the Gallican and the Roman, some kind of cross-fertilization took place. It was a simple matter to impose the texts of the Roman chants, since they were contained in the manuscripts. It was quite a different matter when it came to the melodies. The overall style of the Roman chant, including its modal structure,[6] was in general accepted by the Gallican musicians,[7] but they covered it over with a completely different style of ornamentation—the style to which they themselves were accustomed. In other words, instead of a simple replacement of one by the other, the result was a hybrid that might be formulated by the following equation, in which the arrow represents cross-fertilization:

*Roman * Gallican → Frankish-Roman*

The most ancient musical witness to this cross-fertilization goes back to the end of the eighth century, to the Tonary of Sant-Riquier,[8] which simply indicates the first words and the mode of a few pieces in the new style of chant. A whole century would pass before chant books containing musical notation would appear. The first ones to have come down to us date from the very end of the ninth century, and more especially from the tenth.

Like all the most ancient liturgical chants, the new Frankish-Roman chant repertory was born of the oral tradition, as can be clearly demonstrated by internal analysis. But if we accept the historical hypothesis that has just been described, there must have been a break in the oral tradition: the suppression of one local (Gallican) repertory and its replacement by a foreign one (Frankish-Roman). This imposition of a new repertory on the entire West met with a great deal of resistance in Gaul, in Milan, in Rome itself, and in Spain. Two conditions helped finally to bring about the success of such an upheaval:

- the invention of a system of noting down the melodies in writing, which marks a considerable turning point in the history of music;

- the attribution of the composition of the new chant to one of the most famous figures of Christian antiquity: Pope Gregory the Great.[9]

The composition of Gregorian chant lies within the context of a great movement of civilization, which historians have called the first "Carolingian Renaissance." During this period the barbarian races, which were in the process of establishing themselves, were looking toward the culture of the ancient Greeks and Romans, and they indulged in attempting to emulate the Byzantine Empire. As a result, the new repertory immediately became an object commanding the attention of the musicologists of the time. Those known as the theoreticians would force the various chants into rhythmic and modal categories sometimes far removed from the truth of their original composition. These are the same men, who—as early as the ninth century, in other words, even before the writing of musical notation was fully in place—were to go in for experimentation with syllabication and organum, which would provide the new repertory with unforeseen developments.

NEW COMPOSITIONS AND REFORMS

Seen from the musical point of view, the second half of the Middle Ages appears as a period of intense creativity and theorizing.

The progress of notation

The earliest notations have no indication of pitch intervals, but only of rhythmic values and agogics (variations of expression). This is clearly what was best for a type of music that is essentially a vocal declamation, guided by the extreme freedom of the inflexions of the words. But notation was soon required to find some way of indicating the pitches of intervals. By comparing manuscripts, one can see that this further requirement had the effect of making it impossible to maintain the delicate precision of the rhythmic signs.

The gradual appearance of staff lines, then clefs and the guide, and finally their interconnection within the system of the Guidonian stave (named after Guido d'Arezzo)—all this, while restricting the notator's possibility of showing precisions of rhythm, helped to expand the diffusion of the repertory and to lighten the memory

load. The Guidonian stave, developed during the first half
of the eleventh century, might be compared with a filter
through which to view the original composition. It will
probably prevent us from ever discovering the complete
truth about the primitive scales, with their microintervals
and the practice of *musica ficta*.

ve, etc. Archangé-lica Marí- am fá-
mina salutánti- a   sic fantur : A*ve* *ma*ris, cœli, terræ orbis
renátrix Mar*i-a,* *gra*vida intácta   et Dé- i grá-*ti-* *a ple-na.*
*D*omino summi De- i géni-to altitróno complacu- ísti devó-
ta virgo, íde- o Do- *minus* *tecum,* etc.

—— *Offertory trope* Ave Maria ——

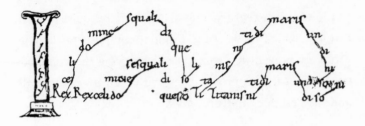

—— *Polyphonic sequence* Rex cæli Domine ——

At its birth, musical notation was intimately tied to oral transmission. Before it came into being, one sang everything from memory. For decades while it was being elaborated, one still sang by heart, but the cantor had recourse to the book to prepare himself before the service. Once the system of notation was established, everyone sang with their eyes glued to the book. Little by little the role of the memory diminished; the singer was no longer able to reproduce the original vocal articulations: he was stopped in his tracks by the inevitable inadequacy of the signs.[10] A new chapter of musical history was about to begin.

> "The loss of momentum in the flow of Gregorian music, caused by fixed restrictive points of phraseology, opened up a new era of creation."[11]

Syllabication of melismas

A melisma, or jubilus, is a vocalization, a moment of pure music that develops over a single syllable; it is a means of elaboration that is essential to Gregorian chant. From the ninth century onward, however, the melismas of certain pieces (Alleluia, *Kyrie*, and others) became the object of *syllabication* with the addition of tropes—that is, extra words, one syllable for each note of the melisma. These tropes, which display both wit and ingenuity, not to mention mannerisms and pedantry, were hugely popular as early as the tenth century.

> "But there was another side to the coin which must be taken into account: when melismas, which were originally purely vocalizations, were transformed into syllabic chants by the addition of words, this modification changed not only the original style, but also contributed to distorting the rhythm; in effect, it resulted in the individual notes, which were often of varying duration as seen in the original notation, ending up being all of the same length when each is pronounced as a single syllable."[12]

Organum

The ninth-century treatise *Musica enchiriadis* contains the first piece of polyphony known in the West, and it lists the first theoretic requirements for music in more than one part. It is obvious that a simple doubling at the fourth totally destroys any sense of the modality of the original single line of melody, whereas the efforts of the performers to keep the parts together spells utter ruin to the flexibility of its rhythm.

After the Council of Trent (1545–1563), Gregorian chant entered upon a period of reforms regarding both editions and performance. The Renaissance and its "humanists"[13] took it upon themselves to make systematic corrections of the melodies, and to subject them to the rules of classical Latin (as they understood them at that time!). The long melismas, which had become tiresome since the art of singing them had been lost, were truncated, being left with only a few notes. The printed editions could offer nothing but "a heavy, boring succession of square notes, incapable of inspiring a single feeling and saying nothing to the soul."[14]

THE RESTORATION IN PROGRESS

In 1833, a young priest in the diocese of Le Mans, Prosper Guéranger, undertook the task of restoring the life of Benedictine monasticism to the priory of Solesmes after forty years of interruption due to the

French Revolution.[15] The Rule of St. Benedict describes the monastic day as being entirely centered around the solemn celebration of the Mass and the Divine Office. To restore the Benedictine way of life meant therefore a return to the liturgical forms of Christian antiquity. Dom Guéranger was not particularly musical, but he had good taste, erudition, and discernment. Moved by spiritual charisma, he started to work with enthusiasm for the restoration of Gregorian chant.

He began by criticizing his monks' performance of the chant and asked them to respect the primacy of the text, its pronunciation, accentuation, and phrasing, all this to guarantee intelligibility at the service of prayer. After a few years, thanks to the invaluable words of advice of a local priest, Canon Gontier, the singing of the chant in the little monastery was transformed, and news of it began to spread. The first rule of how to interpret Gregorian chant had been stated:

> "The rule that governs all other rules is that, pure melody apart, chant is an intelligent declamation, with the rhythm of speech, and well-phrased. . . ."[16]

Between the years 1860 and 1865, Dom Guéranger put one of his monks, Dom Paul Jausions, in charge of restoring the authentic melodies, in accordance with the following principle:

14

—— *Comparative table* ——
(*Solesmes*, atelier de paléographie musicale)

"If someone honestly believes he has found the true Gregorian phrase in all its purity in a particular piece of chant, it will be when examples of that same piece, from churches some distance apart, give the same reading."[17]

Work began in a very austere way. It entailed copying by hand the most ancient manuscripts of Gregorian chant to be found in the Bibliothèque Municipale d'Angers. Their script, "in delicate 'fly-legs,'" was for the time being indecipherable.

In this effort to rediscover the original shape of Gregorian chant, the abbot of Solesmes was not alone. His work was part of a wider movement of interest in the sacred repertory.[18] It was, nonetheless, at Solesmes that the work of restoration assumed the necessary scientific dimension. The first attempts at comparing a number of manuscripts, undertaken by Dom Jausions, were followed by those of Dom Joseph Pothier, and resulted in 1883 in the publication of a first book of chants for the Mass, in which the restitution had already reached a very creditable level of excellence. It had been preceded by *Les Mélodies Grégoriennes* in 1880, the first treatise on the composition and performance of Gregorian chant. This book is still of value today, having lost none of its relevance.

Dom André Mocquereau developed this scientific enterprise by compiling a collection of facsimiles of the principal manuscripts containing the chant to be found in the libraries of Europe. In so doing, he became the founder of the workshop and publication known by the name of *Paléographie Musicale* (1889).

This collection of facsimiles, enriched by such indispensable tools as catalogues, card indexes, and synoptic charts, constitutes the material foundation for the restoration of the Gregorian melodies.

By the beginning of the twentieth century, this research resulted in the publication of an official edition[19] of chants for the Mass (*Graduale Romanum*, 1908) and for the Divine Office (*Antiphonale Romanum*, 1912).

A further stage was reached with the publication of the *Antiphonale Monasticum* (1934), which shows how much progress had been achieved in this work of faithful restitution.

But this was not to be the final word on the chant: the Second Vatican Council (1963–1965) called for a new and better critical edition of the existing chant books.[20]

To achieve this aim, scholars at the present time have been greatly helped by the work of Dom Eugène Cardine (a monk of Solesmes, 1905–1988). It was he who first discovered the laws of the earliest handwritten neumes. He also laid the foundations for a critical edition of the *Graduale Romanum*. The origins of the Gregorian repertory remain shrouded in mystery,[21] making it impossible in our day to be certain that there exists a single manuscript archetype of this repertory, a unique and totally reliable source of all the documents that have come down to us. All we can look for is a source used for the diffusion of the repertory. The publication of this critical edition cannot therefore be envisaged within the short term. However, we now know which are the most important witnesses of the tradition: they are catalogued and studied; they are gradually revealing their secrets.

The word "restoration" deserves to be understood in its totality. To improve the basic shape of the melodies is already a step in the right direction toward the restoration of Gregorian chant. But this restoration will be fully achieved only when Gregorian chant is firmly integrated into the normal, living practice of the liturgy by the whole assembly (in monasteries, parishes, etc.). There are indeed some entire communities that are working hard at this restoration of the practice of the chant, but quietly, unobtrusively, and with no musicological pretensions whatsoever. . . .

2

LITURGY

*The Church acknowledges Gregorian chant
to be the music that belongs specifically
to the Roman liturgy.*

VATICAN II

The Roman Catholic liturgy makes great use of the chant. Many actions of its public worship (processions, for example) are accompanied by chants. At certain moments the ritual act is reduced to a single line of text sung either by a solo voice or by the whole assembly (the chant between the readings, for example). Since chant is so closely linked to the liturgy, it is obvious that a study of Gregorian chant requires a thorough knowledge of the liturgy.

The heart of the liturgy is the celebration of the Mass, or Eucharist. In this sacred action the Church, solemnly gathered together in the diversity of her members, through the ministry of priests renews the actions and words of Christ on the evening of the Last Supper, the day before He freely offered Himself up to death for the salvation of mankind. For the last two thousand years, in obedience to the explicit command of Christ,[22] the Church has never ceased to reenact these gestures,[23] and it is in their accomplishment each Sunday that she passes them on to us. It is because the sacred chant is intimately bound up with this celebration, clothing it as with a garment, that we can understand how this very repetition of the liturgical action itself has passed the chant down to us.

Everything spread from Jerusalem, where the Church was founded, and from Antioch, where for the first time the disciples of Jesus were called Christians.

The celebration of the Lord's Supper was an innovation that marked a radical departure of Christian worship from that of Judaism. However, if the first Christians quickly distanced themselves from the sacrificial practices of the Temple, they were the heirs to a great deal of Jewish ritual practice.[24] For example, the morning Synagogue worship on the Sabbath, made up of Scripture readings, chants, Scriptural commentaries, and prayers,[25] is the origin of the first part of the Mass, the only difference being that the celebration took place on Sunday[26] to commemorate the Resurrection, instead of on Saturday. It added in the Christian texts that make up the New Testament, paving the way for a whole new liturgical creativity, which led, in its turn, to strong apostolic clarification.[27]

Christian liturgy also includes the Liturgy of the Hours, or the Divine Office. This collection of prayers marks the different moments of the day, resulting in nothing less than the sanctification of time. The cycle of the Hours was itself gradually elaborated as it developed from its Jewish origins.[28] Even though this daily prayer affects every Christian, it is in monasticism that it finally took shape. The Rule of St. Benedict (ca. 530) exercised a decisive influence in this organization. There are two major celebrations in the daily structure: Lauds in the morning and Vespers in the evening; daybreak is anticipated shortly after midnight by the long service of Vigils (Matins), in which readings (from the Bible, the Fathers of the Church, and the lives of the saints) have pride of place. As the day goes on, the community reassembles for the "Little Hours": Prime[29] in the early morning, Terce at about ten, Sext at the end of the morning, None at the beginning of the afternoon, and Compline just before bedtime.

For St. Benedict, the Divine Office was above all a service of praise:

> "Let us therefore, during these moments, offer
> up our praise to our Creator . . . and let us rise
> again in the night to praise Him. . . ."[30]

The singing of psalms and the readings from Holy Scripture constitute the main part of the repertory, but St. Benedict also allows for poetic, nonscriptural texts (hymns) and other ecclesiastical writings (litanies, special blessings, and collects) to be included.

22

VIII
MBCKS

C Antémus Dómino: glorióse enim honorificátus est: equum et ascensórem proiécit in mare: adiútor et protéctor factus est mihi in salútem.

℣. Hic Deus meus, et honorábo eum: Deus patris mei, et exaltábo eum. ℣. Dóminus cónterens bella: Dóminus nómen est illi.

—— *Paschal Vigil* ——
Canticle to follow a reading from the book of Exodus

THE BASIC LITURGICAL UNIT

Tertullian, at the beginning of the third century, offers us an eyewitness description of the structure of the Sunday liturgy:

> "There are readings from the Scriptures, the chanting of psalms and the preaching."[31]

Thus Tertullian furnishes us the framework for what could be called "the basic liturgical unit":

reading—chant—prayer

This outline might be placed in parallel with the titles of those taking part and the books they use:

reading	lector	*lectionary*
chant	cantor	*cantatorium*
prayer	priest	*sacramentary*

That same structure has remained intact to this day in the first part of the Easter Vigil.

This succession *reading—chant—prayer* is repeated seven times. After the third reading one can still see how the canticle grows naturally out of the reading itself.

We can recognize in this an archaic musical form, that of the *lectio cum cantico*: both reading and chant are performed by the same singer, because at that time (second to third century) the vocal participation of the assembly was fairly limited, amounting probably to little more than a few simple acclamations in response to the celebrant and his ministers.

The succeeding centuries were to add new rituals, resulting in the completion of the solemn Mass of the eighth century,[32] without disturbing this basic structure, which was to remain as a fine tracery underlying all subsequent ceremonial development (see p. 26).

THOSE TAKING PART IN THE CELEBRATION AND THEIR INDIVIDUAL ROLES

In a solemn liturgical celebration, the assembly is organized according to the diversity of its members. Each one of them has his particular part to play.[33] The chant has adapted itself to this situation. It provides whatever in the repertory is best suited to the ability of each.

The celebrant

Through his sacramental ordination the priest has received the power to sanctify and to instruct the faithful. It is he who presides over the assembly, but he is not trained to undertake any specifically musical or elaborate vocal part. His repertory therefore is restricted to an extremely sober style. The quasi-syllabic cantillation covers a limited range, and any slight variations in pitch only amount to a simple punctuation of the text. These inflections are easily memorized; they are repeated day after day and have come down to us purely by oral transmission. Simplicity is by no means poverty: nothing is lacking aesthetically in these cantillations. Did not Mozart himself once write that he would have given his entire output of compositions for the glory of having composed the melody of the Gregorian Preface?

The people

The assembly replies to the words of the celebrant and his ministers with short acclamations in the same extremely simple style. A popular repertory was gradually established, made up of chants for the Ordinary of the Mass (*Kyriale*), hymns for the Divine Office, and some processional chants.

The schola cantorum

The *schola* is the group of cantors, that is, the group of more vocally gifted and more experienced singers who place their musical talents at the service of the sacred celebration, thereby fulfilling a truly liturgical ministry.[34] The repertory of the *schola* is made up of more elaborate chants. It covers the processional chants, namely the introits, offertories, and communions.

The real vocal specialists, the solo cantors, are to be found among the members of the *schola*. The most difficult and highly elaborate Gregorian chants are reserved for them:

MASS	VESPERS & LAUDS	MATINS	LITTLE HOURS
Introit + Psalm *Kyrie* *Gloria* Collect	℣. *Deus in adiutorium*	℣. *Domine labia mea* Invitatory Hymn	℣. *Deus in adiutorium* Hymn
	Antiphons & Psalms	Antiphons & Psalms	Antiphons & Psalms
READING Lessons	Short Lesson	Long Lessons	Short Lesson
CHANT Gradual Chant Tract Alleluia	Short Responsory Hymn Versicle	Great Responsory *Te Deum* & Its Verses	Versicle
[Gospel	Gospel Canticle	Gospel]	
PRAYER General Intercessions Prayer	Litany *Pater* Collect	Short Litany *Pater* Collect	Short Litany *Pater* Collect
Offertory Canon – *Sanctus* *Pater* *Agnus Dei* Communion + Ps. *Ite missa est*	*Benedicamus* *Domino*	*Benedicamus* *Domino*	*Benedicamus* *Domino*

N.B. This table must be understood as *an archeological and pedagogical outline, not a theological one.* It is clearly a prayer that informs the whole celebration, in particular the Canon.

D̶ Ominus vo·bíscum ℟. Et cum spí·ri·tu tu·o.

℣. Sursum corda. ℟. Habémus ad Dómi·num. ℣. Grá·ti·as

agámus Dómino De·o nostro. ℟. Dignum et iustum est.

V̶ E·re dignum et iustum est, æquum et sa·lu·tá·re, nos

ti·bi semper et u·bíque grá·ti·as á·ge·re: Dómi·ne, sancte Pater,

omnípotens ætérne De·us: per Christum Dóminum nostrum.

Per quem hódi·e commérci·um nostræ repa·ra·ti·ó·nis efful·

sit, qui·a, dum nostra fra·gí·li·tas a tu·o Verbo suscípi·tur,

humána mortá·li·tas non solum in perpé·tu·um transit honó·

rem, sed nos quoque, mirándo consórti·o, reddit ætérnos.

Et íde·o, cho·ris angé·li·cis so·ci·á·ti, te laudámus in

gáudi·o confi·téntes:

—— *Preface from the Mass for Christmas* ——

the chants that come between the readings. Everyone sits and listens attentively to what amounts to a "musical homily."

So the Gregorian repertory presents itself to us as being intimately bound up with the liturgy of the Roman Church. At the time when the Fathers of the Church were explaining Divine Revelation by rhetorical and literary means, another commentary on Divine Revelation was being elaborated, one that was both lyrical and musical, a "musical patrology."

3

PSALMODY

*The psalm was recited with such
minute inflections that this recitation
was more like speech than chanting.*

ST. AUGUSTINE[35]

The traditional and ancestral way of passing on any sacred teaching, as can be seen in those religions that venerate the Bible, and also in many other cultures, has been given the technical name of *cantillation*. This neologism, invented a century ago,[36] indicates a style in which the text takes precedence over the music, whereas the role of the music is both to control and to add solemnity. It is a type of declamation that lies halfway between speaking and singing, for the purpose not of adorning the text, but of enhancing the word.[37] Cantillation lights up the words, enabling them to carry further and with greater significance than if they were just spoken: it lends them a very specific character, in keeping with the priestly nature of a sacred place. From the moment they are heard, they bring to mind another world, and they generate the appropriate *ethos* for acts of worship. But their musical substance remains rudimentary to such an extent as to be hardly worthy to be called chant.

I N-ci-pit Lamentá-ti- o Je-remí- ae Prophé-tae.

A-leph. Quómodo sedet so-la cí-vi-tas plena pópu-lo :

facta est qua-si vídu- a dómi-na Génti- um : princeps pro-

vinci- árum facta est sub tri-bú- to. Beth. Plo-rans plo-

rávit in nocte, et lácrimae e-jus in ma- xíl-lis e-jus : non

est qui conso- lé-tur e- am ex ómni-bus ca- ris e- jus :

omnes ami-ci e-jus spre-vé-runt e- am, et facti sunt e- i

in-imí- ci.

—— *Holy Week* ——
A reading from the Lamentations of Jeremiah

It is in a context of this type of "stylized declamation"[38] that we should situate the birth of Western chant, a context somewhat akin to that of the solemn oral instruction of a group, at a time when the faithful were unable to read.

THE MUSICAL FORMS OF CANTILLATION

The musical material of cantillation is extremely limited: its range is usually restricted to a few degrees of the scale, hardly ever exceeding the range of a fourth. One of these degrees has the function of the principal note, the others ornaments. But the term *ornament* must not be taken to be equivalent to the meaning it came to have in the later musical tradition. The ornaments—*agréments*—of Baroque music have the appearance of being superfluous. The ornaments of cantillation, on the other hand, are an essential part of it. They can be consecutive or contrasting, just occasionally ornamental, their function being to throw the principal note into relief and make it possible to identify the modal structure. All the musical substance is directed toward the text: ornamentation is at the service of the word or the sentence; the rhythm is that of solemn declamation.

This musical enhancement of the text is achieved in three ways:

1) by accentuation
2) by punctuation[39]
3) by the jubilus

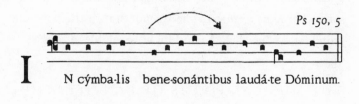

Ps 150, 5

IN cýmba·lis bene·sonántibus laudá·te Dóminum.

—— *The melodic shape of the Latin word* ——

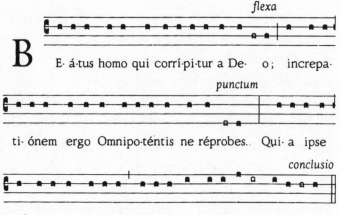

flexa

BE· á·tus homo qui corrí·pi·tur a De· o; increpa-

punctum

ti· ónem ergo Omnipo·téntis ne réprobes.. Qui· a ipse

conclusio

vúlne·rat et medétur, pércutit, et manus e·ius saná· bunt.

—— *The reading tone for the lessons of the Divine Office* ——

In actual fact, only analysis can reveal these differences. They are not entirely independent of each other: the last two are closely intertwined.

Accentuation

The languages of the Mediterranean basin tend to be singsong by nature, with something approaching a pitch accent. Cicero even mentions that this was so in the case of ancient Latin: he speaks of a *cantus obscurior* in words, a latent, hidden melody.[40]

In Gregorian cantillation this characteristic manifests itself by a tendency to raise the pitch of the accented syllable; in musically elaborated chants the word even ends up as a perfect arching phrase of melody.

This is the phenomenon of the *accentus* (from *ad cantum*: "for the chant"); the accent, "the soul of the word and seed of musical art,"[41] governs a whole new musical creativity. For there exists a true dynamism in the Latin word: the word is an evolving melody. The accented syllable rises in pitch, and this is counterbalanced by the final syllable descending to a structural note.[42] The other syllables are carried along by this movement: those preceding the accent are a preparation for the highest point; those following are a transition toward the ending. All this happens within the unity of a single rhythmic entity, that of the word.

Punctuation

Punctuation is an integral part of speech. In the first place, it is of vital importance to the reader, who can accomplish his task only if he is able to take a breath, which demands of necessity a brief interruption in the flow of words. It is equally important for the listener. He is led to a full understanding of the chanted lesson by the whole range of pauses, phrase endings, and caesuras, skillfully used by the reader.

Besides, is not silence also itself a part of music? Is it not the breath, the life of music?

In point of fact, several centuries before the invention of notation, the first signs to appear in the manuscripts were those relating to punctuation. They show the reader minor pauses, more important breaks, and major ones; questions were often shown by a special sign. These early musical indications, which go by the name of *ekphonetics*, bear witness to the existence of an oral tradition that tended to place these caesuras at a lower vocal pitch, or more precisely at the degree of the scale immediately below the reciting note. As can be seen from a study of the pentatonic scale, this pitch is situated a second or a minor third below the pitch of cantillation.

The practice of lowering the pitch for the ending became more elaborate in the reading tones and was itself an additional factor—corresponding to the rise in pitch for the accent—contributing to the development of Gregorian chant.

We hope you will enjoy this book and find it useful in enriching your life.

Book title: _____

Your comments: _____

How you learned about this book: _____

Why did you buy this book? _____

If purchased: Bookseller _____ City _____ State _____

I would like to know more about: _____

Name _____

Email _____

Visit www.paracletepress.com
to receive our newsletters, read more about our books
and other products, and to receive promotional discounts.

PARACLETE PRESS
PO Box 1568 • Orleans, MA 02653 • 1-800-451-5006

PARACLETE PRESS
PO Box 1568
Orleans, MA 02653

The Jubilus

The third way leading into musical development, which arose through primitive cantillation, has a particularly archaic appearance: it is the jubilus, or melisma. This represents a moment of pure music, which intervenes in the course of the syllabic recitation. It is in contrast with it, and consists in the unfurling of a vocalization on a single syllable. To quote the unforgettable words of St. Augustine,[43] the chant "cuts itself free from the shackles of its syllables." The jubilus is not, for all that, any less an authentic form of composition linked to cantillation: the jubilus is not a piece of music from which the words have been removed, and which is somehow incomplete: it is a song over and beyond words, beyond those concepts always somewhat constricting that are evoked by words.

The link between the jubilus and the cantillation is purely functional: its traditional position was on the final syllable, before the penultimate logical division of the text.[44] With the passage of time, this traditional position, which goes back to the ancient cantillation of the Jewish Bible, was gradually forgotten. The jubilus gravitated little by little toward the ends of phrases, and in particular toward the verbal accent, seen as the lyrical and expressive pole of the composition.

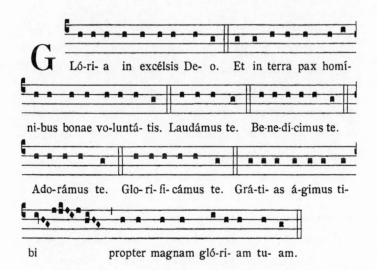

Ló-ri- a   in excélsis De- o.   Et in terra pax homí-

ni-bus bonae vo-luntá- tis. Laudámus te.   Be-ne-dí-cimus te.

Ado-rámus te.   Glo-ri- fi- cámus te.   Grá-ti- as á-gimus ti-

bi   propter magnam gló-ri- am tu- am.

—— *Opening verse of the Ambrosian* Gloria ——

PSALMODY:
ITS MUSICAL SUBSTANCE—ITS FORMS

The basic liturgical unity that we studied in the last chapter has shown us how to recognize the *lectio cum cantico* as the ancestor of Western sacred chant. From the textual point of view, it represents firstly a scriptural canticle, and later a psalm. But what has been the shape, the musical style of this chanting over the centuries?

Psalmody without a refrain (or in directum*)*
There is no easy access to any knowledge about the liturgy of the first two centuries; all we can gather comes

from a number of deductions. During this early period, the chanting of the psalm was not very different from a sung reading. The same minister chanted the reading first, followed immediately by the psalm. The cantillation of the psalm was hardly more elaborate than that of the reading, and followed on naturally from it.[45] This chanting was the part played by the solo cantor, whereas the assembly participated in the liturgy by its prayerful and attentive listening. This state of affairs was appropriate at a time when the faithful had little education and the texts had limited dissemination. The music came from a purely oral tradition: it was a rare commodity. Any musical creativity was the sole preserve of the cantor, and even that went no further than ornamentation.

The shape of the music was adapted to this situation, which was both historical and liturgical. The psalmist went straight through the canticle or the psalm, verse after verse, "in a straight line," or "directly," as it were, with no intervention on the part of the assembly, just like a reading. St. Benedict described this manner of singing the psalm as *in directum*, which today we might translate as to be sung without a refrain.

One can detect the characteristics of psalmody in the melodic shape of an elaborate piece of chant. The reciting notes of cantillation are generally easy to recognize through the three main ways outlined above. There are special melodic formulae for beginnings of verses (intonations), and others for endings (cadences). When the halfway point is elaborated, this gives rise to its own particular formula

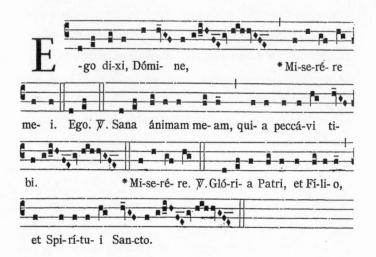

E -go di-xi, Dómi- ne, * Mi-se-ré- re me- i. Ego. ℣. Sana ánimam me- am, qui- a peccá-vi ti- bi. * Mi-se-ré- re. ℣. Gló-ri- a Patri, et Fí-li- o, et Spi- rí-tu- i San-cto.

—— Short Responsory ——
with the melisma in its traditional position

V Ení- te, exsultémus Dómino; iu-bi-lémus De- o salu-tá-ri nostro. Præ- occupémus fáci- em eius in con- fessi- óne, et in psalmis iu-bi-lé-mus e- i.

—— Monastic Night Office of Vigils ——
Verse from the Invitatory psalm

(the mediant cadence). The whole piece usually starts with a solemn intonation, heard only once, and ends with a fully developed formula having a strong tendency toward melismatic treatment (see the example on p. 22).

It is possible to detect the musical form of psalmody *in directum* (without a refrain) in the repertory as it has come down to us, provided we ignore the later ornamentation, which may have obscured it, and above all, those responsible for performing it. This is because those archaic elaborations, originally the preserve of the solo cantor, did, in fact, appear much later, when they were within the competence of the *schola cantorum*.

Taking that into account, we can nonetheless still detect psalmody *in directum* in the Vespers versicle, the Good Friday and the Holy Saturday canticles, and the Lenten tracts.[46]

Psalmody with a refrain (or responsorial)

The next stage of development (third to fourth centuries) is the active participation of the assembly in the psalmody.

There are innumerable historical references to this.[47] They bear witness to the immediate success and dissemination of a new form of Western chant, the responsorial psalm.

In this style, the solo cantor loses none of his autonomy and continues to chant the whole psalm. But at the end of each division, or of each verse, the assembly responds with a short refrain, very easy to memorize, and suggested to them by a cue from the Cantor at the beginning. Thus the oral tradition continues to reign.

The first refrain that came to mind as a possible one was obviously the opening verse of the psalm, or to be more precise, the second half of this verse: so to "respond," for the assembly, came to mean to finish the verse intoned by the cantor. Another refrain that was established right from the start as well, at least on Sundays, was the Alleluia, recalling the Resurrection.

Then the time came when the assembly ceased to respond "automatically" with the first verse of the psalm, and began to look within the psalm itself for a more suitable text, or one more closely linked to the mystery that was being celebrated, or to the liturgical season (the notion of the "chosen verse").

In the Gregorian repertory, it is in the Short Responsory of the Office that the shape of responsorial psalmody can be seen most clearly, even if today the psalm itself has been abbreviated. Some of the Short Responsories have even retained their traditional melisma.

Hidden beneath a cloak of considerable elaboration, we can still see traces of psalmody with a refrain in the A–B–A form of the Gradual of the Mass, and of the Great Responsory of the Divine Office.

The Invitatory chant of monastic liturgy has the appearance of some kind of ancient psalmody without a refrain that has been adapted to responsorial psalmody.[48]

The question of alternation (antiphonal psalmody)

As monastic life began to take shape (fourth to fifth centuries), Christian worship became profoundly influenced by the daily or weekly recitation of the entire Psalter, *per ordinem*, that is, following the order in which the psalms are arranged in the Holy Bible: Psalms 1, 2, 3. . . . Communities of monks and nuns would live by this recitation-*cum*-meditation as they sought to live a life of perpetual prayer. They learned the Psalter by heart, and they possessed manuscript copies of it. The celebration of liturgical worship as laid down by St. Benedict consisted very largely of the recitation of the psalms. The community was divided into two choirs facing each other, and they sang alternate verses.

This alternation fits both forms of psalmody we have seen above. Psalmody *in directum* chants all the verses, one after another, alternating between the two choirs.[49] Alternation can be maintained in psalmody with a refrain, but the two choirs join forces to sing the refrain together after each verse. Over the years, the two choirs ended up singing the refrain together only at the beginning and at the end of the psalm. When this happened, the alternating recitation of the verses was framed by the chant of the refrain. This practice became inevitable once the refrain grew and was further developed musically.

But since at least the time of St. Benedict, there has existed some ambiguity in the terminology.[50] In fact, in the Latin of the Rule for the Monks, the term *antiphona* may be taken to mean either alternation (from the manner in which the chant is performed), or else the refrain of a responsorial psalm: the antiphon.

This verbal ambiguity has led all commentators to suggest that there was a third type of psalmody, to which they gave the name *antiphonal psalmody*. They cite as examples of it the "antiphons" of the Mass (Introit, Communion) and of the Divine Office. But such a distinction would concern the manner of performance, or whoever was to perform it, and not the musical form of the piece being sung. An analysis that really takes into account both aspects, the liturgical and the musical, can, in fact, accept the existence of only two forms of psalmody: that without a refrain (*in directum*) and that with a refrain (responsorial psalmody), both susceptible of being performed either with or without alternation.

The musical destiny of the antiphon

When the refrain became detached from the succession of verses to find itself relegated to the beginning and the end of the psalm, it gradually gained for itself a certain autonomy. The antiphon was soon to present itself, in its own right, as an unequalled open field for musical invention.

From that time on, the term *antiphona* would designate any chant sung with a psalm verse—even such a richly ornamented chant as the Introit.

But the musical career of the antiphon had not come to an end at that point: in the later chant books the word finally came to mean those chants that cannot be included in any well-defined category, even those sung without any trace of a psalm! This includes the famous collection of Marian antiphons, in honor of Our Lady, among which the best known is the *Salve Regina*.

THE THREE ARCHAIC MODES: "BASIC STRUCTURAL NOTES AND MOTHER-CELLS"

The musical substance of cantillation is rudimentary, limited both in its choice of structural notes and in its range. But it is organized. When one examines the most ancient cantillations from the repertories of the Latin West, one finds that they are organized around one particular degree of the scale, the reciting note, in relation to which all the other sounds in the tune are ornamental. In other words, in these primitive melodies, one single degree of the scale assumes the role of principal structural note: it dominates over the whole composition and its ending, eventually becoming the reciting note of the psalm.

Thus, in the Sunday antiphon below, the structural note of the cantillation is found on the degree above the semitone (half-step):

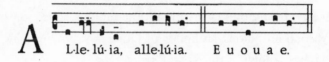

A Lle·lú·ia, alle·lú·ia.   E u o u a e.

In the second example, on the contrary, this structural reciting note has a full tone (whole-step) both above and below:

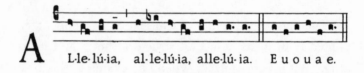

A L·le·lú·ia, al·le·lú·ia, alle·lú·ia.   E u o u a e.

Finally, in this third example, the structural reciting note is placed beneath the semitone (half-step):

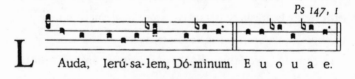

Ps 147, 1

L Auda, Ierú·sa·lem, Dó·minum. E o u a e.

When we examine the facts, we invariably find that the reciting notes used for cantillation always fall into one or other of these three categories. Musicologists have named these three ancient reciting notes "mother-notes," because all ulterior melodic development comes from them.[51] To speak of them in terms of sol-fa is a delicate matter, since they existed several centuries before the invention of note-names, and indeed well before the advent of any musical theory. One cannot, however, avoid it entirely.

If we do try to speak of these three "mother-notes" in the classic terms of solmization, we have DO (C), RE (D), and MI (E); and they can be placed within the context of a pentatonic scale, which lacks the semitone (half-step). It is even possible to schematize the particular structure of each of these archaic modes by revealing a pentatonic "mother-cell" grouping the most important degrees. The detection of the "mother-cell" enables us to identify the corresponding structural reciting note, the "mother-note."

One finally ends up with the following schema:

Mother-note DO Mother-cell   sol - la - DO

Mother-note RE Mother-cell   la - do - RE

Mother-note MI Mother-cell   do - re – MI

MODAL EVOLUTION BY
RAISING THE PITCH OF THE TENOR
(RECITING NOTE) AND THE ACCENTS

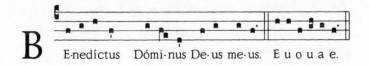

B E·nedíctus Dómi·nus De·us me·us. E u o u a e.

—— Rise in pitch for the psalm of a third above ——
the final of the antiphon

V E-ni- ent ad te * qui detrahé-bant ti-bi, et ado-

rábunt vestí-gi- a pe-dum tu- ó- rum. E u o u a e.

—— Rise in pitch for the psalm of a fourth above ——
the final of the antiphon

THE LAWS OF MODAL EVOLUTION TAKING THE MOTHER-NOTES AS THE STARTINGPOINT

The three archaic modes are the first stage, the basic structure of the Western melodies. Everywhere they underwent an evolution, which led to the development of modality in two directions.

The raising of the pitch of accents and of tenors (reciting notes)

Chants composed using the archaic modality, when sung with a psalm, easily acquired a "tenor" for this psalm higher in pitch than the dominant used in the composition of the chant. The refrain (sung by the people) remained unchanged, whereas the psalm (sung by the solo cantor) came to be sung a third or a fourth higher than the original pitch.

The reason for this evolution may have been the temperament of some soloist keen to show off his fine voice, which shone more at the higher pitch, whereas the people kept their response unchanged. It could also be due to a genuine process of composition. Thus, in the Introits *De ventre* (see p. 78), and *Resurrexi* (*G.T.* p. 196), the tenor of the psalm, which is barely visible in the antiphon, comes as a very welcome contrast to it. The raising of the tenor pitch may also be purely the result of some theoretician's anxiety to integrate the piece into the eight-mode framework of the octoechos.

MODAL EVOLUTION BY LOWERING THE PITCH OF THE FINAL OF THE ANTIPHON

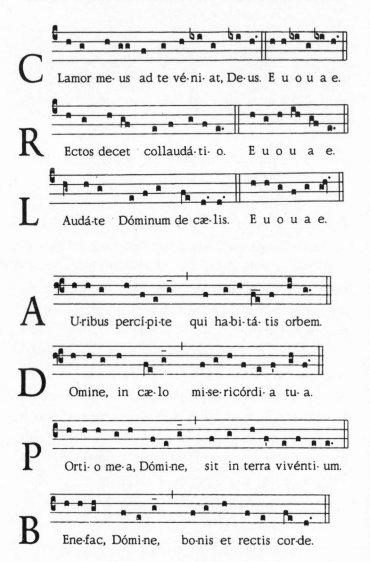

Correlatively with this rise in pitch of the tenors, we can see a tendency toward a raising of the accents to higher degrees of the scale. An internal dynamism develops within the composition, moving upwards, tending to enlarge the intervals.

Such a tendency toward a rise in pitch is well within the nature of the accent: it represents the progressive flowering of the *cantus obscurior* we discussed earlier (see p. 33).

This development involving the ascent of the tenors and accents ends up with the establishment of new modes. These are no longer archaic, yet they remain close to the mother-notes. One might describe them as "ageing."

The descent of the finals

Another evolution moves in a downward direction: much as in speech, the ending of chants tends toward a lowering of the voice (see p. 48):

Antiphon *Clamor meus / Rectos decet / Laudáte*
final   *la*   *mi*   *re*

Antiphon *Auribus / Dñe in cælo / Pórtio mea / Benefac*
final   *si*   *la*   *sol*   *fa*

Bipolar modality and the table of the octoechos

The two phenomena of evolution that affected the ancient melodies are complementary. So to sum it up, the great majority of pieces in the repertory are controlled by bipolar modality.[52]

According to which interval separates these two poles (the dominant of the composition or tenor of the psalm, and the final of the piece), and taking into account the organization of the degrees of the scale within this interval (the position of the semitone [half-step]), it is usual now to assign the piece to one of the modes, designated by numbers or by specific terms elaborated during the Middle Ages (Protus, Deuterus, etc.). In spite of the serious inconveniences that this nomenclature presents, it has been discussed by numerous authors on a grand scale and must therefore be mentioned.

The major problem with the table on page 51 is that it conceals, under a single mode number, pieces having evolved in two distinct ways and which represent in reality two different "modal types."

Antiphon *Dóminus*	mother-note RE
	ascent of tenor to *fa*
	ascent of accents to *fa* and *sol*

| Antiphon *Oblátus* | mother-note DO (= *fa*) |
| | descent of the final to *la* (= *re*) |

		Reciting note of the Psalm		
		THIRD FOURTH plagal modes		FIFTH authentic modes
Final of the antiphon	RE Protus	*fa* mode 2		*la* mode 1
	MI Deuterus		*la* mode 4	*si* mode 3
	FA Tritus	*la* mode 6		*do* mode 5
	SOL Tetrardus		*do* mode 8	*re* mode 7

—— Official table of the octoechos ——

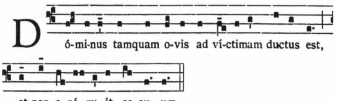

Dó-mi-nus tamquam o-vis ad ví-ctimam ductus est,

et non a-pé-ru-it os su-um.

O blá-tus est, qui-a ipse vó-lu-it, et

peccá-ta nostra i-pse portá-vit.

—— Modal types ——

Both are labeled with the same number (2), because they have the same final and the same tenor; but they clearly represent two distinct modal types within Mode 2 since the dominant note of their composition, and therefore of their aesthetic, is different.

On the other hand, this table makes a distinction between modes that are not completely different from each other, since one can detect "modal equivalences." For example, two antiphons from two different modes might share the same intonation: *Tradétur enim* (Mode 1) and *Quando natus es* (Mode 3).

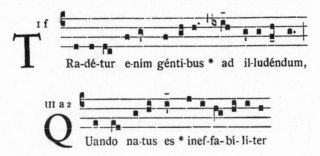

This discovery of "modal types" and "modal equivalences" goes to prove that the table is the work of theoreticians, well after the era of composition. This table, known as that of the "octoechos," fails to take into account the musical facts when these are viewed objectively, but attempts instead to force most of the repertory into a limited straightjacket of categories.

If a study of the different modes and the objective laws of Gregorian modality goes far beyond the scope of these pages of initiation, it will be useful, nevertheless, to devote a few more lines to the underlying structure of this modality: the pentatonic scale.

THE PENTATONIC SCALE AND ITS ORIGINS

The scale that gave birth to Western sacred chant is a pentatonic scale with no semitone (half-step). It is found in the traditional music of many parts of the world: China, Korea, Japan, Vietnam, Mongolia, also in Greek and Hungarian folksong. It probably found its way to us via Indo-European migrants. In addition, all authentic Negro spirituals stem from it, which extends it still further into Western Africa. And finally, it can also be found in Latin America.

In the vocabulary of the musical theoreticians, from Guido d'Arezzo onward, there are three possible ways of notating it:

(Relative pitch)	(Absolute pitch)
sol – la -*- DO – RE – MI -*- *sol – la*	*g–a*-*C–D–E-*-*g–a*
do – re -*- FA – SOL – LA -*- *do – re*	*c–d*-*F–G–A-*-*c-d*
re – mi -*-SOL – LA – SI -*- *re – mi*	*d–e*-*G–A–B-*-*d-e*

There are certainly some pieces of Gregorian chant, from both the Mass and the Divine Office, which are entirely constructed using this scale: the Communion *In splendóribus* (see p. 80), or the hymn *Imménse cæli cónditor.*

Mménse cæ-li Cóndi-tor, Qui mixta ne confúnde-rent,

Aquæ flu- énta dí-vi-dens, Cæ-lum de-dísti lími-tem.

The three degrees in the middle of this scale are the three mother-notes of archaic psalmody, from which emerged the whole of the modal evolution we have been studying.

The two lower degrees are the first finals to which the evolutions of the archaic modality eventually led, through the descent of the final; and the two higher ones are the first higher dominants, reached by the ascent of the tenor.

The asterisk, inserted between the outer notes of the minor third, represents the *pien.* This is a weak, non-structural note of negligible importance, often missing, but which can also make its appearance in a melody. It is mobile—that is to say, it can move either higher or lower within the minor third according to the center of gravity of the melody. This phenomenon is characteristic of the art of song in oral traditions.[53]

It is quite remarkable to see that the earliest musical notations, those with neumes, had, from the very first, special signs to indicate certain details of this scale: the quilisma was used for the weak degree (*piena*), and the stropha for the strong, the one above the semitone (half-step). In the form of notation that finally prevailed, only a single mobile *pien* remained, the B, which can be either natural or flat, two possible positions—in principle mutually exclusive.

The study of the evolution of Gregorian modality, from its earliest manifestations that we have just described up to the establishment of fully developed modes, is going to be, from now on, a whole new area of musicology worldwide, with all the comparisons with other ancient repertories that it invites. It is an integral part of the history of the melodic language of the West.

*

* *

There are innumerable layers of composition in Gregorian chant, from the earliest to the most recent. A large part of the repertory (particularly that of the Mass) was substantially revised by the *schola*, and has been an art of erudition since the sixth century. Then, in the eighth century, all these chants underwent Franco-Roman hybridization. In spite of all, the ancient forms and the archaic scales have left significant traces. That is not the least puzzling aspect concerning the origins of Gregorian chant: the reforming cantors (of the sixth to eighth centuries) had respect for the ancient forms, even though they made adaptations. Oral tradition commands respect!

4

THE DIVINE OFFICE

While they are gathered together in church,
I can think of nothing more useful,
nothing more holy for Christians to do,
than to sing the psalms.

SAINT AUGUSTINE

A study of the Gregorian repertory from the musical point of view as well as from the liturgical one leads to the discovery of two distinct and clearly differentiated groups of chants: the Divine Office and the Mass.

Chants for the Mass appeared in the earliest manuscripts with notation, dating from the tenth century. All over Europe at that time they shared the same texts, the same melodies, and more or less the same rhythmic nuances: they made up a unified repertory, with a monolithic appearance.

The chants for the Divine Office did not appear in manuscripts with notation until after the year 1,000. They hand down to us, however, forms that are much more ancient. Compared with those of the Mass, they form a far less homogeneous group, containing successive layers that bear witness to the evolution of liturgical music. Being subject to diverse local influences, they also display musical and textual variants that are sometimes considerable.

The Rule of St. Benedict, dating from about 530, gives the most precise set of laws that the early centuries have left us concerning the organization of the Liturgy of the Hours. A close study[54] shows that the author, St. Benedict, relies partly on pre-existing usage: that of the Church of Rome. So from very early times there must have been two sources: the Roman (or secular) and the monastic. These two sources would inevitably exert some influence on each other. The substance of the Office has remained the same for both: Scripture readings and psalmody. But their organization is slightly different. Both chant the whole Psalter over a week,[55] but in a different order. They also share the same musical forms. The Rule of St. Benedict, however, gave a generous place to metrical hymns as early as the sixth century, whereas it was only from the thirteenth century that Rome allowed them to be included.

One important difference between the Divine Office and the Mass is the hardly perceptible influence that the *schola* exerted over the musical forms of the Divine Office:

> "The monastic and clerical community is learned from the biblical point of view, but hardly so from the musical one, and nothing can be changed in its daily practice."[56]

This comment should be understood in the context of the earliest monastic communities. It explains why we find both simple and archaic forms witnessing to the oral tradition. At the time of the Carolingian Renaissance, the situation was very different: monasticism was no longer a stranger to musical composition or to musical theory—quite the contrary.

The musical forms of the Divine Office are those of the major forms of psalmody: psalmody *in directum* lies behind the versicle, and responsorial psalmody is the origin of the Short Responsory, of the antiphon used in conjunction with a psalm-tone, and of the Great Responsory with its verse.

THE VERSICLE

The term *versicle*, in the context of liturgy and psalmody, may have a number of different meanings. To be precise, we are using it here to mean the "versicle at Vespers," the shortest piece in the whole repertoire, sung after the hymn and before the *Magnificat* canticle.[57]

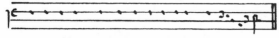

Dirigátur Dómine orátio mea

Everything here points to the antiquity of this piece.

First, the text: "Let my prayer be directed, O Lord, as incense in thy sight." This is the second verse—the most significant—of Psalm 140. In Jewish worship it recalls the evening offering of incense.[58] In Christian worship, the raising of hands for the evening sacrifice (the psalm goes on to mention this) symbolizes Christ's death upon the cross, in the afternoon of Good Friday. There is a remarkable point of contact here between Jewish and Christian worship. Proof exists of the choice of Psalm 140 for the evening service from as early as the end of the fourth century.[59]

Then there is the question of modality. The version in the present editions of the books seems to suggest bipolarity fa–re. But a number of manuscripts have preserved an earlier version, in the ancient RE mode. In some cases the ornamentation is even limited to a bare minimum: to the degrees immediately above and below the mother-note.

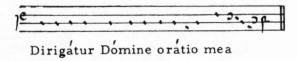

Dirigátur Dómine orátio mea

Finally, the style. This is syllabic recitation on a single pitch followed by a melisma on the final syllable of the last word, an absolutely classic formula found in early chants; in some manuscripts the melisma is even found in the penultimate logical division of the text. It is precisely in this rudimentary form that the canticles of the Paschal Vigil have been preserved in the Beneventan repertory (which is considerably earlier than the Gregorian):

Sic- ut | cervus desiderat ad | fon- tes á- | qua- | rum.

I- ta | de-side-rat anima me- | a ad te | De- | us[1].

Si- ti- | vit anima me-a | ad De- um | vi- | vum.

Quando | veni-am[a] et appa-rebo ante | fa- ci- em | De- | i.

The "Vespers versicle," therefore, represents a particularly archaic musical form in the Divine Office: psalmody *in directum*. Over the years and with other ritual developments, this chanting of psalm 140 has ended up being left with a single verse, the most meaningful one.

THE SHORT RESPONSORY

The second form of psalmody found in the Divine Office is responsorial psalmody. A solo cantor sings the verses, or strophes, and the faithful answer him with a short refrain that is repeated after each verse of the psalm. This form of psalmody with a refrain has been preserved to this day in the Short Responsory (see example on p. 38).

Musical analysis easily distinguishes the part sung by the cantor and that of the faithful. The name *responsory*, traditionally given to this chant, reveals its original form. But this is completely hidden by the manner in which it is sung today, which no longer respects the authentic distribution of roles between the solo cantor and the faithful. Besides, the number of verses has been reduced to a minimum. At a later date, a doxology was tacked on to it (*Gloria Patri, et Filio, et Spiritui Sancto*), the melody of which, evolving toward a higher pitch in the majority of cases, proves well that it was a later addition.[60]

If we leave out of account the added doxology, the Short Responsory still belongs to the category of ancient modality; we can find examples of it for each of the mother-notes.

THE ANTIPHON

When the rules of monasticism prescribed the recitation of the entire Psalter over one week (*psalterium
currens*), it shook the whole structure of the Divine
Office. The primitive forms of psalmody—that have just
been described—were now to be preceded by the chanting of several psalms.

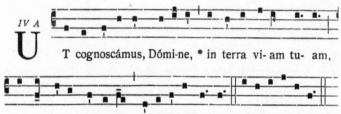

IV A

UT cognoscámus, Dómi-ne, * in terra vi- am tu- am,

in ómni-bus génti-bus sa-lu-tá-re tu- um. E u o u a e.

—— *Antiphon* ——
("typical melody," French mélodie-type, *in Tone IVA)*

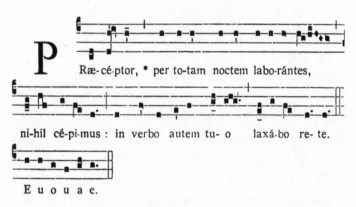

PRæ- cé-ptor, * per to-tam noctem labo-rántes,

ni-hil cé-pi-mus : in verbo autem tu- o laxá-bo re- te.

E u o u a e.

—— *Antiphon composed by centonization* ——

We saw above (pp. 41–42) how this practice sparked off a new musical form: the antiphon. Sung for its own value, it introduces the psalmody and concludes it.

In the huge repertory of antiphons (roughly 4,000 authentic pieces), one can detect several different layers of composition, easily identifiable musically.

The antiphons of the ferial Office (i.e., of the weekday psalmody) are short refrains with a brief text of a few words (generally half a verse) taken in most cases from the beginning or the end of the psalm. Many were still composed using the archaic modality; most of them come from a time when modality had hardly evolved (see pp. 46 and 51).

The antiphons of the ancient feasts are more developed. They are often "melody-types," made up of a few short phrases. Beautifully balanced and perfectly constructed, they are miniature musical masterpieces. Their melodies, without showing any signs of weakness, could be adapted to countless texts.

The third, more recent, layer of composition results from a process of centonization—the piecing together of melodic/verbal formulae, rather like the creation of a mosaic.

Finally, in later compositions, musical invention was given free rein, ending up with madrigal forms or figurative features, announcing the dawn of a new musical era.

64

VIdi * speció- sam sicut co- lúm- bam- ascendéntem désuper ri- vos aquá- rum, cu-ius in- æstimá- bi- lis o-dor e-rat ni- mis in vesti-mén- tis e- ius. * Et sic- ut di- es ver- ni circúmda- bant e- am flo-res ro-sá- rum et lí- li- a convál- li- um. ℣. Quæ est i- sta quæ ascéndit per de- sértum sicut vírgu-la fu- mi, ex aromá-ti-bus myr- rhæ et tu- ris. * Et sic- ut.

—— *Great Responsory* ——
for the Assumption of the Blessed Virgin Mary

THE GREAT RESPONSORY

At the Night Office (Vigils, Matins), readings from the Bible and the Fathers are interspersed with chants: the responsories. There are nine of them in the Roman office and twelve in the Monastic Office.

These chants belong to the category of psalmody with a refrain (responsorial). It is their length that makes them distinct from the Short Responsory. The responsory is made up of two parts: the main part, which is sung by the *schola,* and the verse, reserved for the solo cantor. After each verse, the *schola* repeats the main part of the responsory:

- either in its entirety (Roman use), and this is called *a capite,* an example being the gradual of the Mass;

- or only a part of it (Gallican use—this was called the *réclame*), and this is also known as a repetition *a latere.*

These chants are sometimes highly elaborate, and in that case we can detect in them the influence of the *schola.* Their composition is the product of centonization. But the cantor's part, the "verse" of the responsory, uses a stereotyped melody, the same for every responsory in the corresponding mode of the octoechos. So there are eight of these verse-melodies. They are well-defined melodic formulae, each with its own tenor, intonation, and pentasyllabic cadence. All eight can be easily arranged in a synoptic table. Such systematizing

66

℟.IV

E ce * quómodo móritur iustus, et nemo pércipit corde; et viri iusti tollúntur, et nemo consíderat. A fácie iniquitátis sublátus est iustus; * Et erit in pace memória eius. ℣. Tamquam agnus coram tondénte se obmútuit, et non apéruit os suum; de angústia, et de iudício sublátus est. * Et erit.

—— *Great Responsory for Holy Saturday* ——

of forms and modal conceptions reveals the influence of the theoreticians and makes it possible for us to date the fixing of this repertory to the Carolingian period.

The liturgical situation, the use of centonization, and the ornate style of the Great Responsory bring it close to the Gradual in the Mass. Both, above all, are chants of meditation: contemplative musical commentaries on the sacred text. At the great moments of the liturgical year (Christmas and Holy Week), the chanting of these responsories assumes, to some extent, the role of the chorus in classical Greek tragedy: a running commentary, both lyrical and moving, designed to encourage the participation of the listeners as the drama unfolds.

*

* *

The repertory of the Divine Office, though not so well known as that of the Mass, offers a remarkable summary of the history of Western chant. With its vestiges of the different styles of psalmody, its rather simpler melodies with a modality proceeding in a direct line from their origins, it is an area of predilection for those who wish to start discovering the aesthetics of Gregorian chant.

68

Montes * Gélbo- e, nec ros nec plú-
vi- a vé-ni- at super vos, qui- a in te abjéctus est
clýpe- us fórti- um, clý- pe- us Sa-ul, qua- si non esset un-
ctus ó- le- o. Quó- modo ce-ci-dé-runt fortes in prœ-
li- o? Jóna- thas in excélsis tu- is interféctus est :
Sa- ul et Jónathas, amá-bi- les et de-có-ri valde
in vi-ta su- a, in morte quo-que non sunt sepa-
rá- ti. E u o u a e.

—— *A late antiphon* ——

5

THE PROPER OF THE MASS

Day by day, nourished with bread from heaven,
we say: "Taste and see how good is the Lord."

SAINT JEROME

TRACT AND CANTICLE

The Tract and the Canticle represent the most ancient layer of the chant, that of psalmody *in directum* (without a refrain). In accordance with a law familiar to students of liturgy,[61] they are found at the most solemn moments of the liturgical year: the Easter Vigil and the season of Lent.

The true Canticles of the Easter Vigil are three in number: *Cantemus*, *Vinea*, and *Attende*. Each of them is a scriptural Canticle, not a psalm, being originally linked to a reading according to the schema *lectio cum cantico* (see p. 23). The melody of all three is in Mode 8. One can easily draw a plan of it, and it clearly reveals its psalmodic structure, with its three reciting notes (SOL, SI, and DO), and its special formulae for intonations and both mediant and final cadences. Such a melody, which can be adapted to fit various different texts, is called a "melody-type."

On the Sundays in Lent, we find the Tracts, chants sung between the readings and which belong to the same

70

O cu- li* ó- mni- um in te spe- rant, Dómi-ne: et tu das il- lis e- scam in tém-po- re oppor-tú- no. ℣. Ape-ris tú ma- num tu- am: et imples omne á-ni- mal be-ne-di- cti- ó-ne.

Ps. 144, 15. ℣. 16

GR. VII

—— Gradual, Mode 7 ——

type of psalmody. Not a Canticle, but a psalm sung straight through, verse after verse, with no refrain by the assembly, the Tract was originally chanted by the solo cantor and later by the *schola*.

Tracts have one or the other of two melodies.[62]

One of these, in Mode 8, is a cousin of the melody of the Canticles sung during the Easter Vigil.

The other, classified as being in Mode 2, can be found notably on the First Sunday in Lent, on Palm Sunday, and on Good Friday. This is highly decorated psalmody, with a range of formulae for intonations, and for both mediant and final cadences. It does not, however, fit into the category of the melody-type. It is clearly related to the mother-note RE.

THE GRADUAL

The Gradual is also a chant inserted between the readings. As its authentic title (*responsorium graduale*) indicates, we have here a form of psalmody with a refrain (or responsorial). At first the assembly responded with a simple formula to each of the solo cantor's verses as he went through the psalm. That type of psalmody was usual at the time of St. Augustine of Hippo (end of the fourth century).[63]

But the responsorial psalm was revised and remodeled by the specialist cantors of the Roman *schola* (fifth to sixth centuries). The enrichment of the ornamentation coincided with a shortening of the text. So the psalm was finally reduced to two of its verses: the one chosen for the main body of the Gradual and one other verse. In some cases it is the opening of the psalm that has been preserved.[64] In others, the main part of the Gradual was a verse chosen in order to evoke the mystery being celebrated or to comment upon what had just been read; and so, according to which case, the other verse is either taken from the beginning of the psalm,[65] revealing traces of a more ancient type of psalmody; or it is a continuation of the psalm itself.[66] Sometimes, too, both the main part and the verse look as if they had been specially chosen.[67] In extreme cases, the main part and the verse are chosen from two different psalms![68]

The shape of responsorial psalmody is still present, in its A-B-A form—at least in practice, since one repeats the chant of the main part after that of the verse.

If the composition of the Tracts was limited to those two "ageing" modes, in the case of the Gradual, we have advanced a step further in the area of modal evolution. For the Graduals make use of the four odd-numbered modes of the octoechos: Modes 1, 3, 5, and 7, namely the true authentic modes. To these should be added one family of Graduals, all constructed upon the same melody-type, all clearly deriving from the same mother-note RE: these are the graduals belonging to "the second Mode transposed to *la*."[69] As for the family of 5th-Mode Graduals, it can boast of having about fifty examples, in other words, half of the total number of Graduals.

Apart from that Mode 2 melody-type, Graduals are composed using centonization. This is achieved by selecting from a fund of traditional chants a certain number of formulae that are modally compatible, and piecing them together in the manner of a mosaic, or a "patchwork," so that the resulting chant will fit the shape of the text to be sung. Centonization lies at the heart of the composition of a large part of the Gregorian repertoire, not only of Graduals.

THE OFFERTORY

Of all the chants of the proper, the origins of this one have proved to be the most elusive. The first mention of a chant linked with the Offertory is a comment made by St. Augustine,[70] from as early as the end of the fourth century, about an African church. In view of the close relationship between Northern Africa and Rome, many commentators tend to think that the Offertory chant may have existed in Rome in the fifth century.

In descriptions of the Mass as it was celebrated in the eighth century, the ritual of the Offertory would have been accompanied by a chant performed by the *schola*, like those of the Introit and the Communion. In the earliest chant books, the main part of the chant is followed by several verses,[71] the characteristics of which show without a doubt that they were reserved for the most talented members of the *schola*. As the procession with the offerings became shorter, finally destined to

74

—— Offertory, Mode 4 ——
Prayer of Daniel. Note the final melisma.

disappear altogether, these verses were not retained for any length of time: as early as the eleventh century, they started gradually disappearing from the chant books. At the conclusion of the verses, there was a repeat of a section of the Offertory. Tradition seems also to fluctuate as to the precise placing of this repeat.[72] The Requiem Mass has always retained its Offertory verse, however, up to the present day.

Although this chant has often been grouped together in the same category with the Introit and the Communion antiphons, it differs from them in several respects:

- It comes from a type of chant that is more highly elaborate than either the Introit or the Communion, tending more often to vocalization, especially toward the close.

- Whereas the Introit and the Communion usually display by their texts a clear link either with the liturgical ritual or with the mystery being celebrated, the text of the Offertory, often highly complex in its structure, seems to suggest only a procession or a gesture of offering in a very few extremely rare and even questionable cases.[73] At the high points in the liturgical year and on major feast days, it fits in well with the other texts of the Mass of the day or of the current liturgical season. During the rest of the year, the Offertory, which often uses a psalm text, generally expresses one of the multiple facets of Christian contemplation.

76

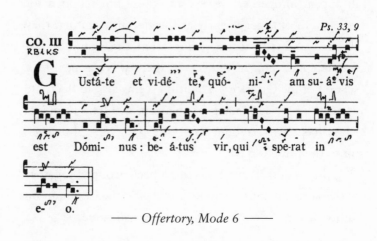

CO. III
RBⱢKS

G Ustá-te et vi-dé- te,* quó- ni- am su- á⸱ vis est Dómi- nus: be- á-tus' vir, qui spe-rat in e- o.

Ps. 33, 9

—— Offertory, Mode 6 ——

IN. VI
RBⱢKS

O mnes gen-tes * pláu-di-te má-ni- bus: iu-bi- lá- te De-o in vo-ce exsulta-ti- ó- nis. Ps. Quó-ni- am Dómi-nus excél-sus, terrí-bi- lis: Rex ma-gnus super omnem terram. Subiecit populos

Ps. 46, 2. 3

—— Introit, Mode 6 ——

There are a few outstanding exceptions, designed on a grand scale, that do not have psalm texts;[74] they are common to other liturgies: *Vir erat, Precatus est Moyses, Oravi, Sanctificavit*, etc.

Some Offertories are not even composed on scriptural texts: *Domine Jesu Christe, Protege*, etc.

The number of Offertories is proportionately smaller than that of either Introits or Communions (about a third fewer), which makes it necessary to repeat the same one for various different moments in the liturgical year. This would be an argument suggesting a certain degree of antiquity for the Offertory.

All these considerations lead us to think that the Offertory does not fit into any category considered "functionary" (like the Introit and the Communion), nor is it a chant belonging to the very essence of the sacred ritual (the chants after the readings, for example). Its role is more that of simply accompanying the ceremonies,[75] of creating an atmosphere through music—vocal music, naturally, taking into account the time when it appeared: a kind of sumptuous "musical offering." A few centuries later it would be the organ that assumed this role.

78

Ē ventre matris meae *

vocávit me Dóminus

nómine meō: et pósuit ōs meum

ut gládium ācútum: sub teguméntō manús

suae protéxit mē, pósuit me quasi

sagíttam eléctam. *Ps.* Bonum est confitéri Dómi-

nō: et psállere nómini tu-o, Altíssi-mē.

———— *Introit for the Feast of St. John the Baptist* ————

THE INTROIT

This chant, a "functional" chant, is sung during the processional entry of the celebrant and his ministers. With this procession, the Introit constitutes the opening rite of the Mass.

This chant witnesses to the importance of the vocal element in the celebration: the unity of the voices invites the faithful to unite, a union that will deepen progressively throughout the celebration.

This chant, which is truly an entrance ritual, plunges us into the mystery about to be celebrated. In the first place by its text, but indissolubly also by its melody, it "sets the tone" of the day, or the feast.

It can be extremely simple, quasi-descriptive:

- *Puer natus est nobis:* Unto us a child is born
  (Christmas)
- *Resurrexi:* I am risen
  (Easter)

Or else, it may suggest a disposition of the soul:

- *Venite adoremus:* Come, let us worship God
  (5th Sunday in Ordinary Time)
- *Ad te levavi:* To thee, O Lord, I lift up my soul
  (1st Sunday of Advent).

80

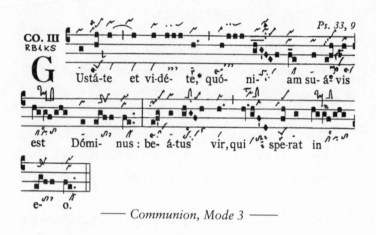

Ps. 33, 9

CO. III
RBLKS

Gustáte et vidé- te,* quó- ni- am su- á- vis est Dómi- nus : be- á-tus vir, qui spe-rat in e- o.

—— Communion, Mode 3 ——

Mt. 26, 42

CO. VIII
RBCKS

Pater, * si non pot- est hic ca- lix transí- re, ni-si bi-bam il- lum : fi- at vo-lúntas tú- a.

—— Communion for Palm Sunday ——

Ps. 109, 3

CO. VI
RBCKS

IN splendó- ri-bus sanctó- rum,* ex ú- te-ro án-te lu-cí- fe-rum gé- nu- i te.

—— Communion for Christmas Midnight Mass ——

The text of the Introit is usually drawn from the Psalms. Sometimes it is taken from another book of the Bible, in which case it often shows that it is closely linked with the readings that are to follow;[76] this is a feature it shares with the antiphon *ad prelegendum* of the Gallican liturgies. A few rare Introits have texts from the Fourth Book of Esdras, highly venerated in the early centuries.[77]

The composer of the Introit respects the sacred text without being a prisoner to it. He makes a choice of the passages he needs, knowing how sometimes to discard any expressions that do not fit into his plan, how to bring together verses that may be far apart, and also how to introduce a word that points out the meaning. In extreme cases, some Introits can be found that sound scriptural though they are not actually from the Scriptures. They are truly ecclesiastical compositions.[78]

There are Introits in all eight modes of the octoechos; this shows that the Introit represents a layer of the chant later than that of the Graduals, and later, with yet stronger reason, in relation to the Tracts.

The Introit is something of a showpiece,[79] an elaborate chant that has been tagged on to the group of antiphons. The singing of it is the preserve of the *schola*, in alternation with the cantor's psalm verses. The chant can be prolonged according to the duration of the procession of the celebrant and his ministers.

This form of chant could make its appearance only once the pattern of solemn worship was well established in the great basilicas. An ancient tradition attributes its introduction to Pope Celestine I (d. 432), but this attribution should be accepted only with a certain degree of caution.[80]

THE COMMUNION

The function of this chant is to accompany the procession of those going up to receive Holy Communion. During the first centuries the majority of liturgical uses in the Mediterranean basin adopted as their text Psalm 33, especially verse 9: *Gustate et videte quam suavis est Dominus* ("Taste and see how good is the Lord"). And so, at this period, the Communion chant never varied at all throughout the year; it was probably sung by a solo cantor, either with or without a refrain from the assembly, according to where the celebration was taking place.[81] The Roman liturgy has preserved the memory of what this verse was to become in the Communion for the 14th Sunday in Ordinary Time: *Gustate et videte* (see p. 80).

When the Communion became the preserve of the *schola,* they chose texts with a Eucharistic bearing, or else directly linked with the particular feast being celebrated that day. The texts were chosen from the Psalms[82] and the New Testament, especially St. John's Gospel.

The Communion chant often has a link with the sacrament that is being distributed. It often, too, tries to establish a close relationship between the Liturgy of the Word and the Eucharistic Liturgy. The best example of this is the Communion *Pater*, from Palm Sunday: "Father, if this *cup* cannot pass from me lest I *drink* it, thy will be done" (see p. 80).

But the choice of text made by the composers is sometimes disconcerting to our modern mentality: the Communions for the weekdays in Lent simply took the psalms in numerical order from 1 to 26!

These compositions use a semi-elaborate style, close to that of the Introits. Like them, they are the preserve of the *schola*, alternating with psalm-verses sung by the solo cantor. When the text is not drawn from a psalm, one can always take the verses from Psalm 33. One finds that the early antiphonaries tend to use the same psalm as that of the Introit, probably from a desire to achieve liturgical unity.

The Communion ritual includes another chant, more especially linked to the *fraction*: the *Agnus Dei*, which belongs to the group of chants known as the Ordinary (see p. 101).

—— *Communion, Mode 1* ——

84

—— Alleluia, Mode 2 ——

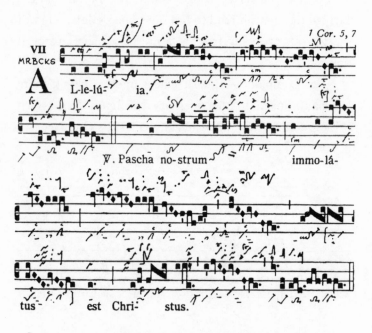

—— Alleluia for Easter Sunday ——

THE ALLELUIA

"Praise the Lord" is a literal translation of the Hebrew word that is common to the heritage of both Jewish and Christian liturgies.

In the earliest manuscripts of Gregorian chant, the Alleluia made its appearance as a chant sung between the readings. In the Mass—for it is also found in the Divine Office[83]—it was originally a chant reserved for Easter Day. From that beginning its use was extended to cover the Paschal season, and then later to the Sundays of the year, a weekly celebration of the Resurrection; but it never penetrated the time of Lent, during which the Tract, a more ancient chant, has stood its ground.

In its definitive shape it represents the most recent of the chants of the proper: the composition of the Roman Alleluias had probably not been completed when the Roman liturgy passed into Gaul in the middle of the eighth century. Their origins are extremely complex. Analysis can, however, reveal three distinct elements in its composition.

- The word *alleluia* itself, usually found with little elaboration, is often a repeat of a syllabic antiphon from the Divine Office.

- Then the jubilus makes its appearance, a vocalization on the divine Name *Yah,* an abbreviation of the ineffable sacred tetragram. This manner of chanting and of exteriorizing one's inner feelings, by a vocalization transcending the limitations of syllables and therefore of concepts, is probably as ancient as humanity itself. Such a chant is admirably suited to function as a preparatory acclamation to the reading of the Gospel, but there is no evidence to suggest that this was its original role in the liturgy; in fact the Hispanic liturgy places it as an acclamation *after* the Gospel.

■ And finally comes the verse, drawn from the Psalms or from another book from the Scriptures (with a few exceptions). This verse, generally unique, represents a lengthening of the original Alleluia chant: a number of early manuscripts have preserved Alleluias without a verse.[84] It is by way of this Scripture verse that the Alleluia has slipped by degrees into the category of chants between the readings.

The ending of the verse is often a repeat of the melody of the jubilus. Sometimes this repeat of the Alleluia after the verse acquired a new jubilus, even further developed: the *sequentia*, *sequela*, or *longissima melodia*.[85]

The Gregorian repertory is made up of three main basic Alleluia melodies, those in Modes 2, 3, and 4,[86] as well as a large number of original melodies.

The late character of the Alleluia chant—in the shape in which it has come down to us—may be detected in a number of different ways.

- The Alleluias are usually found grouped together at the end of the earliest manuscripts: each Sunday the cantor would choose whichever one he wished to sing (*quale volueris*). Tradition had not yet had time to decide this.

- The melodies of Alleluias are often found not to fit the norms of Gregorian composition. They vary from one region to another, a characteristic never found in the other pieces of the Proper.

- The musical inventiveness of the Alleluia is more advanced than that of the other pieces.[87] The existence of musical themes is already well represented, and this foreshadows new musical forms, with repetition, imitation, the opposing and contrasting of melodic motifs, soon to become procedures used in an entirely new sphere of composition.

V E- ní- te, pó-pu- li, ad sacrum & immortá-le mysté-ri- um, & li-bámen a-gén-dum : cum timó-re & fi-de acce-dá- mus; má-ni-bus mun-dis pæni-ténti- æ munus commu-ni-cé-mus; quó-ni- am Agnus De- i propter nos Patri sacri-fí-ci- um propó-si- tum est: ipsum so-lum ado-ré-mus, ipsum glo-ri- fi-cé- mus, cum Ange- lis cla-mán- tes : al- le-lú- ia.

Chant for the fraction *from the liturgy of Lyons*

6

OTHER CHANTS

*The musical tradition of the Universal Church
has created a treasure of inestimable value.*

VATICAN II

The liturgical repertory of the medieval West contains some more chants that cannot be placed in any of the categories studied in the last two chapters. They are mainly the chants of the Ordinary of the Mass and the hymns.

THE ORDINARY OF THE MASS

The celebration of Holy Mass includes certain chants with a fixed text that is independent of the day or the feast. They make up what is known as the Ordinary. They are always called by the first words of the text. These are the *Kyrie*, the *Gloria*, the *Sanctus* and *Benedictus*, and the *Agnus Dei*. We should also include the *Credo*. From the name of the first of these, the whole collection is sometimes known as the *Kyriale*.

In the modern chant books, there is a further grouping into "Masses," collections having a *Kyrie*, a *Gloria*, a *Sanctus* (with *Benedictus*), and an *Agnus Dei*. So we have "Mass I" for Eastertide, "Mass IV" for Feasts of

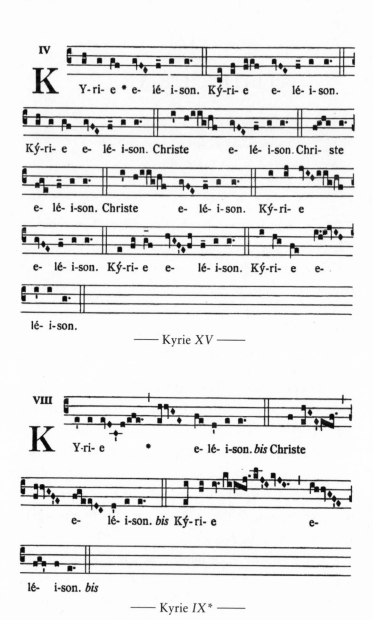

IV

KY-ri- e * e- lé- i- son. Ký-ri- e   e- lé- i- son.

Ký-ri- e e- lé- i- son. Christe   e- lé- i- son. Chri- ste

e- lé- i- son. Christe   e- lé- i- son. Ký-ri- e

e- lé- i- son. Ký-ri- e e- lé- i- son. Ký-ri- e e-

lé- i- son.

—— Kyrie *XV* ——

VIII

KY-ri- e   *   e- lé- i- son. *bis* Christe

e- lé- i- son. *bis* Ký-ri- e   e-

lé- i- son. *bis*

—— Kyrie *IX** ——

Apostles, "Mass XI" for the Sundays of the Year, etc. But we must not be misled by these titles.[88] The labeling dates from the nineteenth-century restoration of Gregorian chant, and it only rarely reflects the historical truth. In fact, the *Kyriale* makes up a composite collection containing a repertory drawn from different regions. Every region at various times composed chants for the Ordinary of the Mass.[89] The number of these compositions goes far beyond the collection that has been passed down to us in the Vatican edition.[90] The choice of pieces in this edition is, however, excellent.

Taken as a whole, these chants are popular in style. Several of them, extremely simple in their composition, could be very old. Unfortunately, tradition cannot be trusted here to the same extent as with the chants of the Proper, and one finds many local variants.

In many cases, though, the influence of the *schola* makes itself felt, producing chants that adopt a much more elaborate style.

The Kyrie

Kyrie eleison (Lord have mercy) is a Greek formula with which the faithful "cry to their Lord, imploring his mercy."[91] This chant, placed today as a penitential rite at the beginning of the Mass, prepares the faithful for the celebration. It was originally an act of praise and a Trinitarian invocation, and was to be found in other places in the liturgy.[92]

In the early manuscripts, the text was written without a break: *quirieleison*, forming a single word. The music has respected this philological component by sometimes developing a sizeable vocalization on the *e* that ensures the junction of the two words, *Kyrie* and *eleison*.

In the Vatican edition, the chant of each *Kyrie* is labeled with a few words in Latin: *Lux et origo*, *Cum jubilo*, *Orbis factor*, etc. This is a relic of the trope that used to accompany the *Kyrie*. Both the *Kyrie* and its trope made their appearance together in the early manuscript tradition. The liturgical reform that followed Vatican II renewed to some extent this ancient link, since it made optional provision for an introductory trope to the *Kyrie*.

When one studies the composition of the *Kyries*, from both the melodic and the modal viewpoints, one can see that very many of them derive from a formula of the archaic MI modality.

The melodic theme *do–re–mi–mi* (or its transpositions) is indeed the basic structural theme of three of the ancient *Kyries*: XV, XVI, and XVIII. It is also an important structural element in *Kyries* III, IX, and X (*Christe*), XI, and I *ad libitum*. It is this theme, too, that opens *Kyries* II, VI, XII, and VI *ad libitum*, and also the *Kyrie* of the Requiem Mass. In *Kyries* I and XVII, this opening theme is obscured by a later rise of a semitone (half-step) *si–do* (or *mi–fa*).

That theme probably stems from the melody of the early Roman litany. In some cases it has managed to retain the true shape of its ancient modality (*Kyrie* XVIII). In others one can easily detect it behind the evolution of the final note toward a lower pitch: the major third (Requiem Mass), or the fifth (*Kyries* II, XI, and XVI). The laws governing modal evolution seem, by analogy, to be equally applicable here (see p. 47). Once again, we can see how the composition of Western sacred music has evolved by stages of a quasi-organic development and has remained faithful to themes and procedures that are genuinely archaic.

The Gloria

This nonscriptural hymn,[93] with no regular meter, is a product of early Christian hymnody. The Latin liturgy has only preserved a few relics of that nature, whereas in the Eastern liturgies it has always had a place of honor.

Both Greek and Syrian sources provide proof of this hymn's existence in the fourth century, and it may come from a second-century Greek original.[94] The Latin text made its appearance in the West in the seventh century and became a regular feature in the ninth. What has been known as the "Greater Doxology,"[95] and which appears in the Milanese liturgy in an even longer version, the *Laus angelorum magna*,[96] was not originally a Mass chant, but a hymn of thanksgiving and jubilation from the end of the Office of Matins.

In the Roman liturgy, the *Gloria* was at first sung at Mass on one occasion only during the year—appropriately, in view of its text, at the Christmas Midnight Mass. Its use was soon extended to include the greatest feasts of the year, but for a while this was restricted to pontifical[97] celebrations. The *Gloria* has now become a chant for the entire assembly, on Sundays (except during Advent and Lent) and feast days.

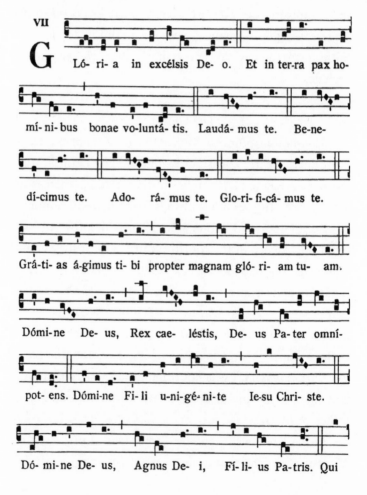

tol-lis peccá-ta mundi,   mi-se-ré- re no-bis. Qui tol-lis pec-

cá- ta mundi,   sús- ci-pe depre-ca-ti- ó- nem nostram.

Qui se-des ad déxte-ram Patris, mi-se-ré- re no-bis. Quóni- am

tu so-lus sanctus.   Tu so- lus Dómi-nus.   Tu so-lus Altíssi-

mus,   Ie-su Chri- ste.   Cum Sancto Spí-ri-tu,   in gló-ri- a

De- i Pa- tris.   A-   men.

—— Gloria *IX, for feasts of the Blessed Virgin Mary* ——

After the intonation, the text has two main sec-
tions: praise in honor of the Father, followed by praise
to the Son. The final mention of the Holy Spirit adds a
Trinitarian note, which sounds like a later addition: this
would suggest a date subsequent to the quarrels linked to
elaboration of the dogma of the Trinity.

The Vatican edition gives nineteen different melodies for this hymn. Two of them stand apart by the simplicity that reveals their archaic character.

The "Ambrosian" *Gloria* (see p. 36) has preserved the style of early cantillation, with recitation on *la* (equivalent to the mother-note RE), its cadences one degree lower, and a jubilus on final syllables, at the penultimate logical division of the text.[98] The final *Amen* differs from the composition of the rest of the piece: it is a later addition.

Gloria XV, also, has kept to the structure of cantillation with *la* as the reciting note (mother-note RE), with a very simple psalmodic formula (intonation–recitation–mediant cadence–final cadence), adapted to fit if the text is too short. The modal evolution is more advanced here (cadences down a fourth), and the final *Amen* is also adventitious.

Other melodies of the *Gloria* adhere to an analogous aesthetic, but not so rigorously.

The mother-note RE can still be easily detected, barely evolved, in *Gloria* XI, II *ad libitum,* and III *ad libitum* (leaps of a fourth and a fifth). In *Gloria* VI, there is some movement toward Mode 8; this modal evolution toward Mode 8 is finally achieved in *Gloria* III (by the ascent of the accents and the reciting notes), and toward Mode 7 in *Gloria* IX (by the descent of the finals).[99]

There is another archaism to be found in the composition of the *Gloria*. Certain passages with a whole series of supplications have often preserved the melody similar to that of the litany that we noticed in the composition of the *Kyrie*. This is particularly visible in *Gloria* XIII, where the theme of the Roman litany in the ancient MI mode appears:

Dómi-ne De- us,   Agnus De- i,   Fí- li- us Patris.

There is a similar theme in the ancient RE mode in *Gloria* XI, which is probably of Gallican origin.

The Credo

This is the Niceno-Constantinopolitan Creed—in other words the Christian profession of faith, defined during the two great Trinitarian Councils of Nicaea (325) and of Constantinople (381), and promulgated officially (451) on the occasion of the Christological Council of Chalcedon.

The chant of the Creed would have been introduced into the Eastern liturgies in a context of baptism by the end of the fifth century,[100] its place in the liturgy varying according to the region.

In the West, the *Credo* must have been introduced into the Hispanic liturgy toward the end of the sixth century. It entered the Gallic liturgies during the eighth to ninth centuries, but it took its place in the Roman liturgy only in 1014 and then only for Sundays and major feasts.[101] As a latecomer among the chants of the Ordinary, it enjoys a special status.

98

Sanctus, * Sanctus, Sanctus Dóminus De- us Sá-ba- oth. Ple-ni sunt caeli et terra gló-ri- a tu- a. Ho-sánna in excélsis. Be-ne-díctus qui ve-nit in nómine Dómi-ni.

Ho-sánna in excélsis

—— Sanctus XVIII *(weekdays in Advent and Lent)* ——

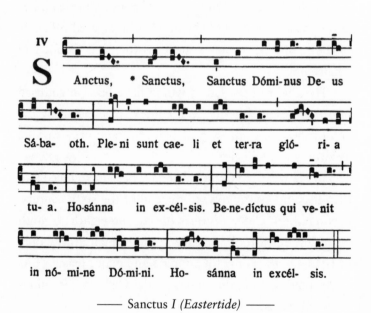

Sanctus, * Sanctus, Sanctus Dómi-nus De- us Sá-ba- oth. Ple- ni sunt cae- li et ter-ra gló- ri- a tu- a. Ho-sánna in ex-cél- sis. Be-ne-díctus qui ve-nit in nó- mi-ne Dó-mi-ni. Ho- sánna in excél- sis.

—— Sanctus I *(Eastertide)* ——

None of the six melodies handed down to us in the Vatican edition departs from the technique of straightforward syllabic recitation. *Credo* I represents the original shape of this chant.[102] Its musical form brings the *Credo* close to a number of prose hymns preserved by the liturgy (notably the *Te Deum* and the *Gloria*). The structure of its cantillation is still clearly visible. As in the psalm-tone known as the *Tonus Peregrinus* (the "wandering tone"), two different reciting notes (tenors) alternate: *la* and *sol*. All the complete phrases make their final cadence on *sol*. Intermediary cadences are made on *mi*, foreshadowing the conclusion on the final *Amen*. The melody is perfectly adapted to the text.[103]

The five other melodies are either repeats of the first (II, V), or later compositions (III, IV, VI), which represent a departure from the authentic norms of composition.[104]

The Sanctus

At the opening of the Eucharistic Prayer, the chant of the *Sanctus* is introduced by the solemn recitation of the Preface. This is the "Hymn of the Seraphim," heard in the Temple in Jerusalem by the prophet Isaiah, during the vision that was to inaugurate his ministry (Isaiah 6:3). It invites the Church on earth to join the heavenly hymnody, manifesting in that way the unity of both liturgies, terrestrial and celestial. This solemn affirmation of the holiness and transcendency of the God of the Universe is completed by an acclamation to Christ the King, taken from the Gospel (Matthew 21:9), and quoting from the Easter psalm (Psalm 117:26).

Among the melodies offered by the Vatican edition, that of *Sanctus* XVIII, at present reserved for weekdays in Advent and Lent and the Requiem Mass, is remarkable for its simplicity. It follows on naturally from the Preface that has just been sung, and leads into the Canon that comes next. What is more, its evolution and its embellishment find their place halfway between those two recitations.[105] It is probably the earliest form of the *Sanctus* to have come down to us.

The fact that this version seems to make its appearance only in later manuscripts in no way weakens that assertion: the simplest chants, those that are sung day after day, were the last to be given written musical notation. At least the first part of the *Sanctus* chant, sung by both priest and people, has been known since the end of the fourth century. The second part (*Benedictus* . . .) was probably added to the Roman Mass in the seventh century.[106]

The other melodies became progressively more elaborate, especially from the eleventh century onward. They offer a whole range of varied compositions, in which practically all the modes are represented.[107] If some melodies (XIII) are roughly syllabic in style, others (II, VII, XI) are much more elaborate.

The repetitions in the text itself called for repetitions in the music and for imitations. Composers did not ignore this invitation (II, III, V . . .), that is, unless they amplified

the whole idea of a direct repeat by juggling with transpositions (XIV).

The Agnus Dei

This is the chant sung during the *fraction* (breaking)
of the Bread that has just been consecrated, in preparation
for the distribution of Communion to the faithful. The
introduction of this chant into the Roman Mass at the
end of the seventh century has often been attributed
to Pope Sergius I, of Syrian origin. Eastern influence is
undoubtedly discernable: *fraction* seen in relation with
the sufferings of the Savior, for example, and also the
designation of the Eucharistic elements as the Lamb.
Now it is well known that the second half of the seventh
century witnessed a massive immigration into Italy and to
Rome of Christians fleeing persecution in the East.[108] But
the *Agnus Dei* was not completely unknown in Rome,
for we can find traces of it, with archaic melodies, in the
petitions of the *Gloria* (see p. 93).

The Milanese liturgy has preserved a chant of the
Proper at this point, a chant that varies throughout
the liturgical year and that goes by the name of the
Confractorium. An analogous chant from the ancient
Gallican liturgy of Lyons has been preserved (see p. 88).
We also know of the collection of antiphons *ad confrac-
tionem panis* from the Hispanic liturgy.[109]

The chanting of the *Agnus Dei* falls to the general
assembly, and it usefully fills the gap between the consecration and the Communion by "greeting with due

homage and humble supplication the One who has made Himself present in the species of bread."[110]

The melody of *Agnus Dei* XVIII, of utter simplicity, is certainly related to the primitive litany. The invocations were repeated for the duration of the fraction. After the introduction of small altar breads and the diminishing participation of the faithful in receiving Communion, the chant was retained but the number of invocations was reduced to three (tenth century), and the concluding *dona nobis pacem* came gradually to be adopted (tenth to eleventh century).

—— Agnus Dei *XII* ——

—— Agnus Dei *XVIII* ——

The textual repetition was generally respected by the composers. Of the collection of twenty *Agnus Dei* settings in the Vatican edition, nine of them have the form A–A–A, nine have A–B–A;[111] only two depart from these forms: *Agnus Dei* VII (A–A–B) and *Agnus Dei* XI (A–B–C). Both of these, however, date from no earlier than the fifteenth and the fourteenth century respectively.

One can see in several *Agnus Dei* chants, notably XII and XVI, that the central invocation has a very simple melody like a psalm tone. This is probably a vestige of the melody of the original litany.

This chant was the last to join the chants of the Ordinary. It brought into being numerous compositions between the twelfth and the seventeenth centuries.[112] It has been given outstandingly sumptuous and solemn treatment. Three of the chants contained in the Vatican edition (III, V, and VI) stand apart as real masterpieces in the history of music.[113]

THE PROSE HYMNS

There are two rather different categories of composition that go to make up the tradition of hymnody: prose hymns and those in verse.

Prose hymns have always met with considerable success in the East, where the tradition of hymn writing has never ceased since Saint Ephrem of Syria.

In the West, only three pieces of this type have come down to us: the *Gloria in excelsis* (see pp. 94–95), the *Te Deum*, and the *Te decet laus*. By contrast, hymns in verse have been given pride of place, especially in the Divine Office.

The Te Deum

The *Te Deum* is a long hymn of praise in prose, sung traditionally toward the end of the Night Office. But its use has been extended to occasions of solemn thanksgiving.

For a century there has been much discussion as to its origin. According to an old legend, the *Te Deum* would have been composed by St. Ambrose and St. Augustine on the day when Augustine was baptized (at Milan in 386). In fact, an analysis of both text and music demonstrates that we have here a composite work that has been elaborated over the centuries by successive additions. Today scholars attribute the final version of this hymn to Nicetas, bishop of Remesiana (the present-day Mediterranean Romania), at the end of the fourth century or the beginning of the fifth.

The first part (up to *Paraclitum Spiritum*) is very similar to a Eucharistic anaphora—that is, praise to the Trinity addressed to the Father. It includes, incidentally, the triple *Sanctus*. The melody is visibly built around the note *la* (mother-note RE), with a slight raising of the pitch of the reciting note (tenor) to the *si*, of the accents to *do*, and dropping to *sol* for punctuation. It is something very close to an archaic modality.

The second part (from *Tu rex gloriæ* up to *sanguine redemisti*) offers praise to Christ the Redeemer. The new text is accompanied by a modification in the melody. The reciting note is still the *la* with accentuation shown by simply raising the pitch one degree higher to the *si*, and punctuation is indicated by dropping to the fourth below, to the *mi*. The verse *Ætérna fac* originally served as the conclusion of the piece.

The third part (*Salvum fac* to the end)[114] represents a further development, both textual and musical. It is a series of petitions, mainly derived from psalm verses. The melody for the most part makes use of the mother-note MI, which can be seen in the mother-cell *do–re*–MI (c–d–E) and in the developments of recitation on *sol*; it occasionally reverts to the melody of the second section.

This section is the least homogeneous of the whole composition, and probably the most recent addition.

H.III&IV

T E De- um laudámus: te Dóminum confi· té· mur.

Te ætérnum Patrem, omnis terra vene·rá· tur. Ti·bi om-

nes ánge· li, ti·bi cæ·li et univérsæ potestá· tes: ti·bi

chéru·bim et sé·raphim, incessábi· li voce proclá· mant:

«Sanctus, Sanctus, Sanctus Dóminus De· us Sába· oth. Ple-

ni sunt cæ·li et terra ma·iestá·tis gló·ri· æ tu· æ.» Te

glo·ri· ó·sus Apostoló·rum cho· rus, te prophetá·rum lau·

dá·bi· lis núme· rus, te mártyrum candidá·tus laudat exér·

ci· tus. Te per orbem terrárum sancta confi·té·tur Ecclé-

107

si- a, Pa-trem imménsæ maiestá- tis; vene-rándum tu-

um verum et únicum Fí-li- um; Sanctum quoque Pa-

rácli-tum Spí-ri- tum. Tu rex gló- ri- æ, Chri-ste. Tu Pa-

tris sempi-térnus es Fí-li- us. Tu, ad libe-rándum suscep-

tú-rus hómi- nem, non horru- ísti Vír-gi-nis ú-te-rum. Tu, de-

vícto mortis acú-le- o, ape-ru- ísti credéntibus regna

cæ-ló- rum. Tu ad déxteram De- i sedes, in gló- ri- a

Pa- tris. Iudex créde-ris esse ventú- rus. Te ergo quǽ-

sumus, tu- is fámu-lis súbve-ni, quos pre-ti- ó-so sángui-ne

redemí- sti. Ætérna fac cum sanctis tu- is in gló-ri- a

108

nume·rá· ri. ¶ Salvum fac pópu·lum tu·um, Dómi·ne, et

bénedic he·re·di·tá·ti tu· æ. Et re·ge e· os, et ex·

tólle illos usque in æ·tér·num. Per síngulos di· es be·

ne·dí cimus te ; et laudámus nomen tu·um in sǽcu·lum,

et in sǽcu·lum sǽcu·li. Dignáre, Dómine, di· e isto

sine peccáto nos custodí· re. Mi·se·ré·re nostri, Dómi·ne,

mi·se·ré·re nostri. Fi· at mi·se·ricórdi· a tu· a, Dómine,

su·per nos, quemádmodum spe·rá·vimus in te. In te,

Dó·mine, spe·rá· vi : non confúndar in æ·tér· num.

———— *Hymnus Te Deum: Tonus antiquus* ————

The Te decet laus

The *Te decet laus* is a short prose hymn that serves as the final ending of the monastic Night Office (Vigils) on Sundays and feast days. St. Benedict borrowed it from the East: it is actually the hymn that concludes the nightly psalmody in the Byzantine liturgy.[115]

Today's chant books contain two melodies[116] for the *Te decet laus*. The authentic melody is the one given for Eastertide. The other is a late adaptation by the Benedictine Monks of the Congregation of St.-Maur (seventeenth century).

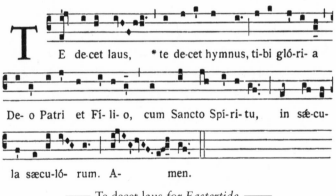

—— Te decet laus *for Eastertide* ——

THE VERSIFIED HYMNS

The importance of hymns in Western liturgy was brought to the fore by the liturgical reform that followed the Second Vatican Council. Now and in the foreseeable future, all the services of the Divine Office can begin with the chanting of a hymn, whereas in the early Church the place of the hymn would vary from service to service. In other words, it is the hymn that "sets the scene" and helps the faithful to enter into the liturgical season or the mystery that is being celebrated.[117] This particular feature of hymns is accentuated by their popular style. They are often fairly simple compositions, extremely easy to sing. The repetition of the same melody for every verse, too, makes it even easier to memorize the music, and this helps to remember the text. Since the earliest times they have played a considerable part in the teaching of orthodox doctrine, as well as in disseminating heretical ideas. . . .

St. Ambrose

St. Ambrose was a writer of hymns: a few of his have come down to us.[118] The future Pope Celestine I, during a visit to Milan, even told us that he had seen how St. Ambrose would get the faithful to sing the *Veni Redemptor gentium*.[119] These hymns were probably composed at a time of struggle against Christological heresies. The simplicity of their meter gained for them immediate success.

It was doubtless because their text was not scriptural that hymns made their official entry into the Roman liturgy only at a much later date (thirteenth century). But monastic rules, such as those of St. Benedict or St. Caesarius of Arles, were quick to welcome them.

The Carolingian Renaissance

The Carolingian era signaled a return to the forms of Greco-Latin antiquity. Many hymns were composed at that time using the classical meters of the ancient Latin poets. Curiously enough, it was above the strophes of the Odes of Horace that the earliest forms of neume notation made their first appearance.[120] This movement of composition was to develop largely in the monasteries, where hymns had been included in the Divine Office since the sixth century. But secular poets have also added their names to the composition of hymns. This leads us to think that, little by little, the singing of hymns must have spread to ordinary churches well before their official adoption by the Roman liturgy. The hymnal, which was more or less established during the Carolingian era, has nevertheless continued to develop right up to our own time.[121]

The composition of hymns

Meter, that is, the organization of the text into long and short syllables and the fixed positioning of certain caesuras, and similarly, the regular repetition of an identical meter for different texts, sets hymns in a category apart in the very heart of Western sacred music. Hymns obey specific rules, close to those of classical versification: they disregard the free rhythm of declamation, which is a fundamental characteristic of Gregorian composition.

The relative indifference of the melody with regard to the text makes it difficult to determine the age of these pieces, at least from the musical point of view. It would be necessary for an ancient hymn—and that hymn only—to be found everywhere and always with the same unique melody, for us to be able to think that it was the "authentic" melody (the original one). But has this ever been the case? Can the very idea of an original melody have any meaning for these compositions, which might even have originated as popular songs? Whatever the answer may be, musical notation made its appearance only in the tenth century, and this makes it impossible to reach any safe conclusion.[122]

Iambic dimeter

Ambrosian hymns normally have eight stanzas (more commonly "verses") of four lines each. Every line has eight syllables, alternating short-long. This is known as iambic dimeter. When it really is a case of quantity that differentiates the syllables (brevity and length), one speaks of a metrical hymn. But in many cases quantity was disregarded, and composers have contented themselves with the regular return of the accented syllables: these are called rhythmic hymns.

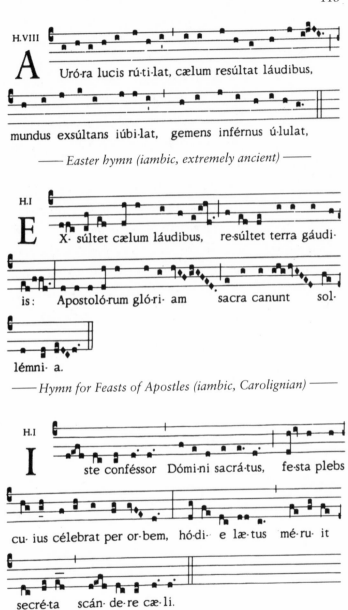

H.VIII

A Uró·ra lucis rú·ti·lat, cælum resúltat láudibus,

mundus exsúltans iúbi·lat, gemens inférnus ú·lulat,

—— *Easter hymn (iambic, extremely ancient)* ——

H.I

E X· súltet cælum láudibus, re·súltet terra gáudi·

is: Apostoló·rum gló·ri· am sacra canunt sol·

lémni· a.

—— *Hymn for Feasts of Apostles (iambic, Carolignian)* ——

H.I

I ste conféssor Dómi·ni sacrá·tus, fe·sta plebs

cu· ius célebrat per or·bem, hó·di·· e læ·tus mé·ru· it

secré·ta scán· de· re cæ· li.

—— *Hymn for the Feast of St. Martin (sapphics)* ——

Sapphics

This meter was much used during the Carolingian era, because it is a classic meter for Horace. The stanza is made up of three lines of eleven syllables, with a caesura after the fifth, and it ends with a line of five syllables (the adonic line). Sometimes bringing together words that would be far apart in ordinary prose speech, this last line gives, as it were, a neat little summary of the whole. In these hymns quantity clearly has a decisive role; the melody often points out the long syllables. But here again the form has evolved, and certain stanzas that use sapphics have ended up with melodies that are independent of quantity, and this then brings them more into the category of compositions that use free rhythm.

—— *Manuscript Worcester, F.160* ——
(English antiphonary, thirteenth century)

7

MANUSCRIPTS

*Notation, far from being the
final goal of musical science,
is not even a part of it.*

ARISTOXENES

By the end of the eighth century, composition of the Gregorian repertory came to an end. This whole corpus of music containing the chants of the liturgical year was born into a context of oral tradition. But as we have already seen (see p. 7), it also occasioned a rupture with preexisting oral traditions. In fact, the Carolingian sovereigns imposed the use of Gregorian chant on their entire empire. In order to achieve this *tour de force*, to overturn one musical tradition and to impose another, it was necessary for those promoting it to invent a system of notating the music.

Mediterranean antiquity had indeed already known ways of writing down and theorizing about music, vestiges of which have come down to us.[123] But the Latin Church had never made use of such knowledge for its chants. The learned bishop and musicologist Saint Isidore of Seville bore decisive witness to this in the sixth century:

118

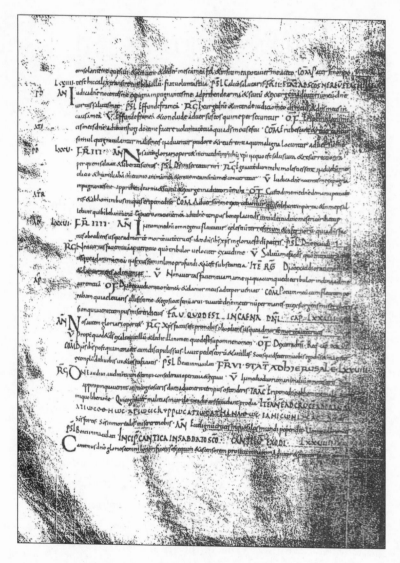

Manuscript Paris BNF lat. 12050
(Graduale *from Corbie, end of ninth century*)

"If the sounds are not memorized by man they vanish, because there is no way of writing them down."[124]

It would take nothing less than a century to produce a system of musical notation suited to the Roman-Frankish repertory. This was a first step—the most important one—toward producing the form of notation we use today.

The end of the eighth century was to witness the appearance of the first collections of manuscripts containing the chants of the Mass. These books still give only the texts of the chants, and sometimes even only the *incipit*.[125] Musical notation had not yet been invented: singers were still bound to follow a purely oral tradition as regards the music.[126]

The most ancient manuscripts of this kind have been edited in the form of a synopsis in the *Antiphonale missarum sextuplex*,[127] a book that is a source of reference for a study of the original tradition. A piece is usually referred to as being "authentic," meaning that it comes from the earliest "Gregorian" repertory, when its text is to be found in the best of the *Sextuplex* manuscripts.

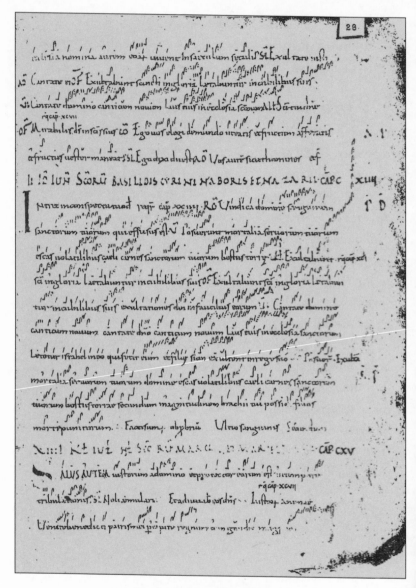

—— Graduale *from Mont-Renaud* ——
(tenth century, French neumes)

THE FIRST GENERATION
OF MUSICAL NOTATION: NEUMES

We find in sources from the second half of the ninth century the first attempts at noting down the music. These are marginal scribbles, neumes oddly placed over the strophes of classical poetry, or the musical examples given by the theoreticians. They have been called "paleo-Frankish"[128] notations.

Then, as early as the beginning of the tenth century, the first notated book of chant made its appearance: the *Cantatorium* of St. Gall. It contains only the chants of the solo cantor (the chants between the readings). The way it is written is pure perfection, both as regards its rhythmic precision and also the beauty of the calligraphy: it can never be equaled. It is a sophisticated form of *aide-mémoire,* for both rhythm and expression, but the melody is still reliant on the oral tradition. This continuing existence of an oral tradition is of extreme importance if we are to understand the full significance of the emerging notation. Precise as it may appear to us—and in this it far exceeds anything modern notation can reveal about rhythm—it is not the foundation of the work. The musical composition itself precedes it by several decades, possibly by more than a century, and independently of any written notation.[129] The early notations might be described as attempts to report on some event: they are trying to show on the parchment the

Manuscript Rome, Angelica 123
(Italian Graduale, *eleventh century)*

inflexions of the voice. They are in no way the written project of a composition that would need to be created[130] through performance, which is the system we have had now for several centuries. The relationship between the composer and the notation used to write it down was fundamentally different then from what it is today.

Of necessity these early attempts had their limitations. In the first place, they were guided by the musical notions of those who were elaborating a system of notation; but they were also guided by the ears and perception of the early scribes, who were not all on the same wavelength. Music, of its essence, is not intended to be written down; it will always transcend any system of notation, however perfect:

> "Certain basic elements of music cannot therefore be written down, or at least, if one does manage to express them more or less exactly in writing, they cannot be reproduced from the written page. The process of writing them down has rendered them sterile."[131]

Moreover, the proof of the limitations of this emerging system of writing down music is that in the course of the tenth century other forms of notation would flourish, many and varied. In about 930, the *Graduale* from Laon presented the complete repertory of Mass chants in "Lorraine" notation (otherwise known as "Messine," i.e.,

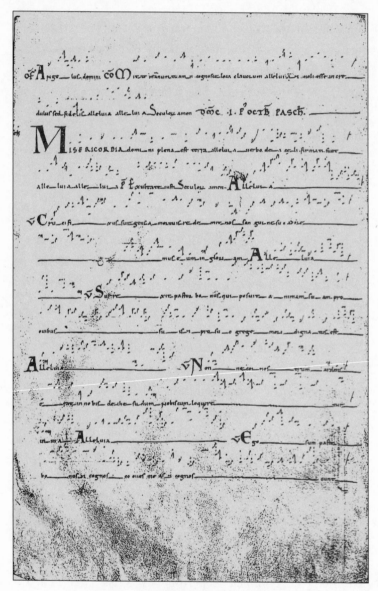

—— *Manuscript Paris, BNF lat. 903* ——
(*Aquitainian* Graduale, *eleventh century*)

from Metz), representing the eastern part of France. As early as the tenth century, Brittany had its own system of writing music: "Breton"[132] notation. The parts of France that lie between Normandy and Lyons also had their own particular neume notations, known as "French" ones, the most ancient of which being the manuscript from Mont Renaud (second half of the tenth century, cf. p. 120). Then there are several tenth-century documents that display a style of notation peculiar to the southwest of France, a style destined to enjoy a rich development, the so-called "Aquitaine" notation.

THE SECOND STAGE OF MUSICAL NOTATION: DEVELOPMENT OF THE STAVE

So the tenth century, with a written repertory of Gregorian chant, is the century that gave birth to musical notation. Every system has its limitations, but there is one limitation common to them all: although they take particular care to offer details of rhythm and expression, they have no way of showing exact pitch intervals. These are notations *in campo aperto* (meaning "in an open field"), also known as "in pure neumes."

A number of these systems, notably those from Lorraine, Brittany, and Aquitaine, already showed some attempt to indicate the relative pitch of the sounds.[133] In the eleventh century, however, these diastematic notations, together with a system of solmization, finally reach a stage of perfection. It is a simplification by historians to attribute the invention of the stave to Guido d'Arezzo. This genius of a teacher brought to perfection the system of staff notation and presented his work to Pope John XIX,[134] who expressed great interest in it; its instigator thus became known to posterity. In point of fact, the stave itself had been gradually establishing itself. Medieval sheets of parchment had lines ruled on them: in other words, horizontal lines were traced on them in advance to facilitate the writing. In order to leave enough room for the scribe charged with adding in the musical notation, it became usual to write the text only on every second line. The empty line would inevitably come to serve as a very useful guide for drawing the neumes horizontally. Manuscripts from all over Europe show us how this line came to be chosen for spatial reference, and how scribes began to write the high notes above it and the low notes below.[135] A single line was enough so long as the writing was done carefully and the melody covered only a small range. When the range was extended, other ledger lines could be added. It is a fact that most of the Gregorian repertory, with its modest vocal range, can be comfortably written down using a stave of only four lines.

The guide is a sign placed at the end of a line in order to show the pitch of the first note on the next stave. It made its appearance during the second half of the tenth century in Aquitaine and in southern Italy.

Clef signs were the next item to appear. Their function is to show the relationship between a theoretical scale and a concrete system of lines by indicating the relative position of the tones and semitones (whole-steps and half-steps) in the diatonic scale.[136] At this stage in the development of musical notation, the influence of the theoreticians would seem to have been decisive, if not preponderant.

Since the emphasis was to be on pitch from this time on, the evidence shows that the scribes begin to adopt a more casual approach to the finer shades of rhythmic subtlety, which had been the main concern of those of the previous century. The writing got coarser: in France the little squares got progressively thicker, and *Hufnagel* (hobnail) notation appeared in Germany. So long as an oral tradition prevails (which is possible in conservative centers such as monasteries), the harm is not irreparable. But once the memory falters, recourse to the book can only spell out the melodic shape of the chants, which are thus deprived of the living, vitalizing sap of their rhythm. A break with tradition was inevitable.

THE END OF THE ELEVENTH CENTURY

These two systems of notation (neume notation and staff notation), which follow one another chronologically, seem on the surface to link up in a logical way. In point of fact they differ profoundly and essentially.

The neume (pneuma) is like a symbol, a projection of the vocal inflexions upon the parchment.[137] Its aim

128

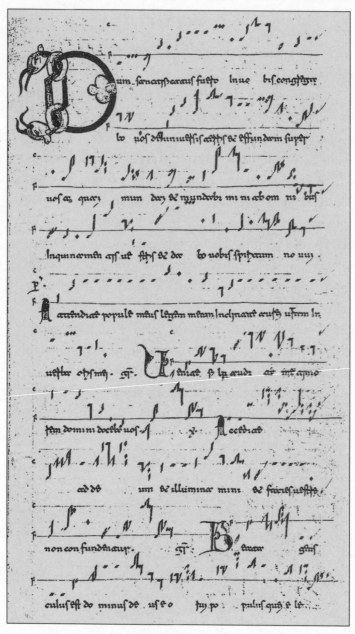

—— *Manuscript Benevento 34* ——
(Beneventan Graduale, *eleventh–twelfth century)*

is mimesis, to draw a picture of the musical reality, and to place before the eyes a sign directly accessible to the imagination:

> "Basically the intention of the system is to translate the melody through gestures and to fix the gesture on the parchment. In reality the neume is a 'gesture in writing.'" [138]

Staff notation, particularly once clefs have been integrated into the system, is based on theory:

> "It does not represent the music itself, but the theory of it . . . the signs correspond to a certain ordering, to relationships understood and formulated mathematically, as established by the theory." [139]

Basically, it was the whole relationship between the singer and his music that had changed; and this probably marks the most important turning point in the entire history of Western music.

In addition, it should not be assumed that the use of these two systems of musical notation was uniform and appeared simultaneously all over medieval Europe. Certain Germanic centers held on to their neume notation until the very end of the Middle Ages, whereas other regions were only too eager to adopt the stave as early as possible. In both cases we have every reason to believe that the "Old Roman" repertory was transcribed directly using staff notation, without the intermediary of neumes *in campo aperto*,[140] while as for the Hispanic repertory, it never showed any signs of a transition from neumes to staff notation.

*

*   *

To gain any idea in our own day of the authentic sound of the Gregorian repertory requires, therefore, that we place, side by side, the melodic version (in staff notation) and the information we are given in the most ancient manuscripts with neumes (Saint-Gall, Laon, etc.). This forms the basis of a new area of study: Gregorian semiology.[141] If one discounts their individual limitations, a comparative study of different manuscripts allows one to rediscover the rhythmic and expressive meaning of the neume notations. By doing so one is able to grasp, to some extent at least, the concrete *actio canendi* that the written signs have tried to freeze onto the parchment. For there are so many things, let it be said once more as we end, that writing is incapable of telling us: pronunciation (use of the voice and articulation), accentuation, what scales were used, microtones, and the vocal technique of another period. Then, of course, we must also take into account the ten centuries of musical civilization that separate us from the mentality of the scribes who were the first to use written notation.

PRINCIPAL ABBREVIATIONS
USED IN THIS BOOK

D.A.C.L.: *Dictionnaire d'archéologie chrétienne et de liturgie*, Paris, 1907.

E.G.: *Études grégoriennes*, Solesmes, 1954 . . .

G.T.: *Graduale Triplex*, Solesmes, 1979.

P.G.: *Patrologia græca*, Migne, 1857 . . .

P.L.: *Patrologia latina*, Migne, 1844 . . .

P.M.: *Paléographie musicale*, Solesmes, 1889 . . .

R.G.: *Revue grégorienne*, Solesmes, 1911–1963.

NOTES

1 In particular, the allusions to the *Liber pontificalis,* a sort of chronicle describing the successive pontificates of the early Church. The *Liber pontificalis* was published by L. Duchesne (Paris: *Bibliothèque des Écoles d'Athènes et de Rome,* vol I, 1886; vol. II, 1892); it was republished by E. de Boccard in 3 volumes in 1955 and 1957. It has been shown, subsequently, with what historical caution one should read the entries (Peter JEFFERY, *art. cit. infra*).

2 These books, intended for the priest celebrant, contain the principal prayers (collects and prefaces) for every Mass in the liturgical year.

3 Certain books, the *Ordines romani,* give detailed descriptions; cf. Michel ANDRIEU, *Les Ordines romani du haut Moyen Age,* 5 vols., (Louvain: 1931).

4 The earliest of them has been published in facsimile by Max LÜTOLF: *Das Graduale von Sancta Cecilia in Trastevere* (Cologne-Genève: Fondation Martin Bodmer, 1987).

5 Philippe BERNARD, "Sur un aspect controversé de la réforme carolingienne: 'Vieux-romain' et 'Grégorien,'" *Ecclesia orans* anno VII-1990/2, 163–89.

6 That is, the main structural points, the principal cadences, and the important recitations and vocalizations.

7   A large part of the repertory shows that the Old
    Roman and the Frankish-Roman pieces are in fact
    very similar. There are exceptions that are being
    studied at the present time.

8   Paris, BNF lat. 13159. Cf. Michel HUGLO, *R.G.*
    31 (1952): 176, 224.

9   This attribution was made all the easier by the fact
    that St. Gregory was supposedly the author of the
    Sacramentary (the book containing the prayers
    of the celebrant), in which the liturgical ordering
    coincided with that of the Roman antiphonary
    of the Mass; but more than a century had passed
    since the official establishment of the so-called
    "Gregorian" Sacramentary and the elaboration of
    the chant merger that bore the same name.

10 The oral tradition continued to flourish, however,
    in spite of the shortcomings of the notation. Just
    as neumatic notation was able to hold its own in
    certain Germanic regions until the fifteenth century,
    so also an authentic interpretation was able to con-
    tinue here and there, even though the melodies had
    been consigned to the stave.

11 Marie-Elisabeth DUCHEZ, "Des neumes à la
    portée," *Notations et séquences* (Paris: Honoré
    Champion, 1987), 60.

12 Dom Eugène CARDINE, "Vue d'ensemble sur le
    chant grégorien," *E.G.* 16 (1977): 184.

13 José DA COSTA RODRIGUEZ, *Les répercussions
    humanistes sur le plain-chant* (essay for a master's
    degree in musical education, under the direction of

Edith Weber, Paris: Sorbonne, 1975 [duplicated by Roneo]. Contrary to a familiar legend, Palestrina cannot be blamed for all the mutilation inflicted upon the Gregorian repertory. (Dom Pierre COMBE, *Histoire de la restauration du chant grégorien* (Solesmes: 1969), 9).

14 Dom GUÉRANGER, lettre d'approbation à la méthode de chanoine Gontier, *op. cit. infra,* xiii.

15 Dom Louis SOLTNER, *Solesmes et Dom Guéranger (1805–1875)* (Solesmes: 1974).

16 Chanoine GONTIER, *Méthode raisonée de plainchant (*Le Mans: 1859), 14.

17 Dom GUÉRANGER, *Institutions liturgiques,* vol. 1 (1840), 306.

18 Lambillotte, Nisard, Danjou were all working in the same area.

19 Commissioned, promulgated, and printed by the Holy See, this edition is currently known as the "Vatican Edition."

20 Constitution *Sacrosanctum Concilium* (1963), 117.

21 Especially when trying to discover how the ora tradition was transferred to the page of manuscript.

22   "Do this in memory of me" (Luke 22:19).

23 *Sacrosanctum Concilium,* nn. 6, 106.

24 The book of the Acts of the Apostles shows that the distinction between the two religions happened only gradually: for a long time Christianity appeared to be just a Jewish sect, with the synagogues of the Diaspora providing the early network of evangelization in the Mediterranean basin (Acts

13:5, 14). See also the resolutions taken by the first "Council" of Jerusalem (Acts 15).

25 On this question, see first Israël ADLER, "Histoire de la musique religieuse juive," *Encyclopédie des Musiques Sacrées* vol. 1, (Paris: Labergerie, 1968), 469–93. Then, for the relationship between Jewish chant and Christian chant, Solange CORBIN, *L'Église à la conquête de sa musique* (Paris: 1960), 52–70; and Eric WERNER, *The Sacred Bridge*, 2 vols. (New York: 1959, 1984), sometimes considered controversial.

26 The French word for the first day of the week, "Dimanche," comes from the Latin *dominica die*: the Lord's Day.

27 Cf. 1 Corinthians 11:17–34 and 14:26–39.

28 The book of Acts shows us Peter and John going up to the Temple to pray at the ninth hour (Acts 3:1).

29 This office made its appearance later than the others, for purely monastic reasons. The liturgical reforms that followed on the heels of the Second Vatican Council (1963–1965) ignore it completely.

30 *Règle des moines*, ch. 16.

31 *De anima*, IX, 4.

32 This ordering of the Mass has been preserved in documents that go back as far as the eighth century. Cf. ANDRIEU, *op cit. supra*, and Dom Jacques FROGER, *Les chants de la messe aux viiie et ixe siècles* (Desclée & Cie., 1950).

33 Instruction *Musicam sacram* (March 8, 1967), nn. 5, 6, 11.

34 *Sacrosanctum Concilium,* n. 29.

35 On the subject of how to sing as laid down by St. Athanasius, *Confessions* X, 33.

36 Solange CORBIN, "La cantillation dans les rituels chrétiens," *Revue de Musicologie* 67 (July 1961): 5.

37 Solange CORBIN, *L'Eglise à la conquête de sa musique* (NRF Gallimard, 1960), 43.

38 Jacques VIRET, *Le chant grégorien* (L'Age d'homme, 1986), 65.

39 Marie-Noël COLETTE, "L'intervention musicale dans le Haut Moyen-Age: ponctuation et transposition," *Analyse musicale* 18, 1er trimestre (1990): 7–17.

40 "Speech contains a latent melody . . . for nature has inserted a higher pitch into each word" (*De oratore* XVII, XVIII).

41 *Anima vocis et seminarium musices,* in the well-chosen words of Martianus Capella (fifth to sixth century); cf. Dom Paolo FERRETTI, *Esthétique grégorienne* (Desclée et Cie., 1938; 2nd ed., Solesmes: 1989), 9.

42 Jean JEANNETEAU, "Style verbal et modalité," *R.G.* 36 (1957): n. 4, 117.

43 *Enarrationes in psalmos* 32, 1.8; 99, 4. One should remember that in these texts, St. Augustine is speaking of responsorial psalmody, not that of the Alleluia.

44 Mgr. E.T. MONETA-CAGLIO, *Lo jubilus e le origini della psalmodia responsoriale,* ed. Jucunda

Laudatio (Venice: S. Giorgio Maggiore, 1976–77); Dom Jean CLAIRE, "La place traditionnelle du mélisme dans la cantillation," *Yuval,* vol. 5, (Jerusalem: 1986).

45 In some manuscripts the reader is warned of the passage from the reading to the canticle by the rubric: *Hic mutes sonum (Here you change the tune). Cf. P.M. t. XX,* tables p. 37*.

46 Dom Jean CLAIRE, *Le répertoire grégorien de l'office. Structure musicale et formes* (Colloque Internationale de Musicologie, Louvain: September 25–28, 1980). Olivier CULLIN, "Le répertoire de la psalmodie *in directum* dans les traditions liturgiques latines," *E.G.* 23 (Solesmes, 1989): 99.

47 The most important one comes from the pen of St. Augustine, in his commentary upon the Psalms.

48 St. Benedict certainly seems to be thinking of two possible ways of singing this: *cum antiphona* (with a refrain), *aut certe decantandum* (or else, as if it were a *cantus* = a straight line, i.e., without a refrain) (*Rule* ch. 9, 3).

49 This type of psalmody still exists, notably in the Office of Compline (*Rule* ch. 17, 9).

50 Dom Jean CLAIRE, *Le répertoire grégorien, op. cit.,* 44.

51 Dom Jean CLAIRE, "L'évolution modale dans les répertoires liturgiques occidentaux," *R.G.* 40 (1962): 236.

52 This is a simplification for the purpose of teaching. There do also exist cases, more complex ones, showing a dual evolution, both an ascent of the tenor and a descent of the final; or else a cascading descent of the final by stages, etc. Cf. *R.G.* 40 (1962): 243, and *R.G.* 41 (1963): 25.

53 The word *pien* comes from the Chinese language: it is used for the two notes that transform the traditional Chinese pentatonic scale into a scale of seven notes. Joseph YASSER, *A Theory of Evolving Tonality* (New York: American Library of Musicology, 1932), 34.

54 C. CALLEWAERT, *Sacris erudiri* (Steenbrugge: 1940; Adalbert de VOGÜÉ, *La Règle de saint Benoît,* vol. 5 (Paris: Le Cerf, 1971), 433.

55 The Psalter covers a period of four weeks in the present-day secular Roman Rite.

56 Dom Jean CLAIRE, *Le répertoire grégorien*, *op. cit. supra,* 34.

57 A similar versicle is sung at Lauds and at Vigils.

58 A mention of this is made at the beginning of St Luke's Gospel.

59 St. John Chrysostom, *Exp. in Ps. 140, P.G.* vol. 55, col, 426–27.

60 Amalarius (ca. 835) claims that it was added by recent popes (*De ordine antiphonarii,* vol. 3, part 1, ch. 1, n.13; *Studi e testi* 140, 1950).

61 "The ancient forms hold their ground most tenaciously at the most sacred seasons of the liturgical year," A. BAUMSTARK, *op. cit. infra,* 29.

62 D. FERRETTI, *op. cit. supra,* 135, 139.

63 Mgr MONETA-CAGLIO, *op. cit. supra,* ch. 1.

64 *Ecce quam bonum* (*G.T.* 351), *Bonum est confiteri* (*G.T.* 327).

65 *A summo* (*G.T.* 27), *Haec dies* (*G.T.* 196), *Juravit* (*G.T.* 486).

66 *Universi* (*G.T.* 16), *Timebunt gentes* (*G.T.* 265).

67 *Audi filia* (*G.T.* 406), *Viderunt omnes* (*G.T.* 48).

68 *Tollite hostias* (*G.T.* 272).

69 Bernard RIBAY, "Les graduels en II A," *E.G.* 22 (Solesmes, 1988): 43–107; and Dom FERRETTI, *op. cit. supra,* 162–74.

70 "Let them chant at the altar hymns taken from the Book of Psalms, either before the Offering, or when they are distributing to the people what has been offered" (*Retractations,* II, 11). This remark has been quoted by all the commentators since the seventeenth century, but it tells us practically nothing, since it refers to a lost work of Saint Augustine. See Joseph DYER, "Augustine and the 'hymni ante oblationem' The Earliest Offertory Chants?" *Revue des Etudes Augustiniennes* 27 1-2 (Paris, 1981): 85–99; and on the subject of Saint Augustine's work, *Œuvres de Saint Augustin,* trans. Gustave Bardy, vol. 12 (Paris: Bibliothèque Augustinienne, 1950), 469, 579, n. 45.

71 Between one and four depending on the pieces, their performance perhaps depending upon the length of the procession (Joseph-André JUNGMANN, *Missarum sollemnia* [Paris: Aubier, 1952], vol. 3, 302 n. 18). The

aesthetic and the ornamentation also appear to vary from one verse to another within the same offertory.

72 Such a type of repeat would link the offertory chant with responsorial psalmody.

73 *Reges Tharsis* (*G.T.* 58), *Sicut in holocausto* (*G.T.* 299), *Domine Deus* (*G.T.* 401).

74 They may possibly be Gallican in origin. Cf. Kenneth LEVY, "Toledo, Rome and the legacy of Gaul," *Early Music History* 4 (Cambridge: 1984), 49–99.

75 Is this not precisely what the post-Vatican II liturgical books have been promulgating? When the offertory is not sung, it is omitted, purely and simply (*General instruction of the Roman Missal* [1969] no. 50), something that never happens to the entrance chant.

76 For example: *Puer* (*G.T.* 47), *Viri Galilæi* (*G.T.* 235).

77 *Requiem* (*G.T.* 669), *Accipite jucunditatem* (*G.T.* 243).

78 *Ecce advenit* (*G.T.* 56), *In excelso throno* (*G.T.* 257).

79 Joseph-André JUNGMANN, *op. cit. supra,* vol. 2, 73.

80 DUCHESNE, *Liber pontificalis,* vol. 1, 230; Peter JEFFERY, "The Introduction of Psalmody into the Roman Mass by Pope Celestine I (422–432): Reinterpreting a Passage in the Liber Pontificalis," *Archiv für Liturgiewissenschaft* 26 (1984): 147–65.

81 See table of liturgical uses in H. LECLERC, *D.A.C.L.*, vol. 3, col. 2428–433, article "Communion."

82 Of the 130 ancient Communions, only 64 have texts drawn from the Psalms, a smaller proportion than from the other categories of chant.

83 Dom Jean CLAIRE, "Aux origines de l'Alleluia," *Essays in honor of Edith Gerson-Kiwi, Orbis musicæ* 9 (Tel-Aviv, 1986): 17.

84 Chartres 47 (tenth century), in particular: *P.M.* vol. 11, 116–18.

85 Cf. "L'alléluia *Redemptionem* et les *longissimæ melodiæ*," *E.G.* 24 (1992): 203.

86 Published in the synoptic tables of *E.G.* 21 (1986).

87 D. FERRETTI, *op. cit. supra,* 182–90.

88 Dom Dominique CATTA, "Aux origines du Kyriale," *R.G.* 34 (1955): 175.

89 Michel HUGLO, "Origine et diffusion des Kyrie," *R.G.* 37 (1958): 85.

90 Collections of these melodies exist. Cf. Mgr Ferdinand HABERL, *Le Kyriale Romanum, Aspects liturgiques et musicaux* (Rome: Pontificio Istituto di Musica Sacra, 1981).

91 *General instruction of the Roman Missal,* no. 30.

92 At the end of the Offices in the Rule of St. Benedict.

93 Except for the opening words, which come from the Gospel for Christmas Midnight Mass (Luke 2:14).

94 *Apostolic Constitutions* VII, 47. Mgr. MONETA-CAGLIO, *op. cit. supra,* ch. 8.

95 To distinguish it from the "Lesser Doxology" (*Gloria Patri, et Filio, et Spiritui Sancto* . . .) attached to the ends of psalms and responsories, as a reminder to venerate the Blessed Trinity.

96 A complete transcription of it may be found in *P.M.,* vol. 6, 316, and in Mgr. MONETA-CAGLIO, *op. cit.,* 165.

97 L. DUCHESNE, *Origines du culte chrétien* 5th ed., (Paris: 1920), 176.

98 This arrangement can still be detected, at least in the first strophe, which is the nucleus of the composition.

99 Here, too, by analogy, we can apply the rules of modal evolution (p. 47).

100 Irénée-Henri DALMAIS, *Liturgies d'Orient*, (Paris: Cerf, 1980), 97.

101 R. CABIÉ, "L'Eucharistie," in A.G. MARTIMORT, *L'Eglise en Prière* vol. 2 (Paris: Desclée, 1983), 149, 162.

102 Michel HUGLO, "Origine de la mélodie du Credo 'authentique' de la Vaticane," *R.G.* 30 (1951): 68–78.

103 See the article by Dom MOCQUEREAU: "Le chant authentique du Credo," *Monographie grégorienne* III (Desclée, 1922).

104 Ferdinand HABERL, *Le Kyriale Romanum, op. cit.,* 177–89.

105 Dom Jean CLAIRE, "L'évolution modale dans les récitatifs liturgiques," *R.G.* (1963): 134–36 and plates **Gc** and **Hc.**

106   Joseph-André JUNGMANN, *op. cit. supra,* vol. 3, 45 n. 41.

107   If Mode 7 goes unmentioned in the rubrics of the Vatican edition, more than one phrase has a suggestion of its aesthetic (notably *Sanctus* I and VII.)

108   Joseph-André JUNGMANN, *op. cit. supra,* vol. 3, 262–63 and notes.

109   "Antifonario vizigótico mozárabe de la Catedral de León" (*Monumenta Hispaniæ sacra liturgica,* vol. 6, t. 2, Madrid, 1953), unfortunately indecipherable as regards the melodies.

110   Joseph-André JUNGMANN, *op. cit. supra,* vol. 3, 263.

111   To be precise, in three cases the form should really be described as A–A'–A, since the second invocation contains a minor variation.

112   The chant melody of *Agnus* II *ad libitum* was composed by Dom Pothier, using a medieval theme.

113   Dom Jean CLAIRE, "Trois mélodies d'Agnus Dei," R.G. 40 (1962): 6–14.

114   Today the singing of it is optional.

115   This Greek hymn may itself have been inspired by a similar piece from the liturgy of the synagogue on the morning of the Sabbath. Cf. A. BAUMSTARK, *Liturgie comparée* (Chèvetogne: 1939), 94.

116   There are also others. Michel HUGLO, "Les diverses mélodies du 'Te decet laus'. A propos du vieux-romain," *Jahrbuch für Litugie und Hymnologie* 12 (1967): 11–116.

117   *General Instruction on the Liturgy of Hours* (1971), no. 173.

118   Pietro BORELLA, *Il rito ambrosiano* (Morcelliana, 1964), 56; M.-H. JULLIEN, "La tradition manuscrite des quatorze hymnes attribuées à saint Ambroise jusqu'à la fin du XIᵉ siècle," unpublished.

119   Peter JEFFERY, *art. cit. supra*, 162.

120   Denis ESCUDIER, "Des notations musicales dans les manuscrits non liturgiques antérieurs au XIIᵉ siècle," *Bibliothèque de l'Ecole des chartes,* 129, (1971): 27–48. Yves-François RIOU, "Codicologie et notation neumatique," *Cahiers de civilisation médiévale* 33 (1990): 255–80, 381–96; "Chronologie et provenance des manuscrits classiques latins neumés," *Revue d'histoire des textes* 11, (1991): 77–113.

121   Pierre-Marie GY, "Le trésor des hymnes," *La Maison-Dieu* 173, (1988): 19–40.

122   Jacques PERRET, "Aux origines de l'hymnodie latine, l'apport de la civilisation romaine," *La Maison-Dieu* 173, (1988): 51.

123   Jacques CHAILLEY, *La musique grecque antique,* ch. 7 (Paris: Les Belles Lettres, 1979).

124   *De musica,* c. 15; *P.L.* 82, col. 163.

125   The term used to designate the opening words of the chant, and taken to mean the whole piece.

126   An indication of modality appears in the ninth century, however, in the margins of the Corbie Graduale (cf. p. 118) when it concerns pieces sung with psalmody (introit and communion).

127 *Antiphonaire missarum sextuplex,* edited by Dom René-Jean HESBERT (Brussels–Paris: Vromant et Cie., 1935).

128 J. HOURLIER and M. HUGLO, *E.G.* 2 (1957): 212–19. K. LEVY, "On the origin of neumes," *Early Music History* 7 (Cambridge, 1987): 59–90.

129 Kenneth Levy, in his article that we quoted in note 128, thinks there may have been one or two attempts at inventing some kind of musical notation during the ninth century, possibly as early as the time of Charlemagne. This more-than-attractive hypothesis is given some emphasis, but requires further study and discussion.

130 This word, which has stood the test of time, may be given its full weight here: before being "created," i.e., "brought to life" through performance, a musical composition has no consistency, in whatever way it may be notated in writing.

131 A. DANIÉLOUP, *Sémantique musicale* (Paris: 1967), p. 27.

132 Sometimes known as "Chartraine," i.e., "from Chartres," because the principal manuscript containing that notation is to be found in Chartres (*P.M.* vol.11). But it was originally from Brittany. For proof, see *E.G.* 1 (1954): 173–78.

133 These systems have prompted the expression "diastematic," either partial or relative.

134 GERBERT, *Scriptores,* vol. 2, 43–44.

135 Cf. Marie-Elisabeth DUCHEZ, "La représentation spatio-verticale du caractère musical grave-aigu et

l'élaboration de la notion de hauteur de son dans la conscience musicale occidentale," *Acta Musicologica* 51 (1979): 54–73.

136 Apart from staff notation, other attempts to show this have existed, in particular alphabetic notation (antiphonary from Saint-Bénigne of Dijon, known as "de Montpellier," *P.M.* vol. 7). This attempt spread throughout the Norman monasteries but was never officially adopted.

137 The expression *chironomique* ("shown by gesture of the hand") has sometimes been used. The term is not without ambiguity, but it has the merit of being evocative.

138 Dom Eugène CARDINE, *op. cit. infra*, 2.

139 Marie-Elisabeth DUCHEZ, "Des neumes à la portée," *Notations et Séquences* (Paris: Honoré Champion, 1987), 58.

140 Guido d'Arezzo's presentation of his system of musical notation to the Pope (John XIX, 1024–1033) is very slightly earlier than the manuscript containing the "Old Roman" gradual in Saint Cecilia in Trastevere. The paucity of rhythmic indications in "Old Roman" manuscripts is entirely symptomatic from this point of view.

141 The foundations of this study were laid by A. Mocquereau, and the scientific importance of it was established by Eugène Cardine: *Première Année de Chant Grégorien* (Rome: 1975) and *Sémiologie Grégorienne* (Solesmes: 1970).

ABOUT PARACLETE PRESS

Who We Are

PARACLETE PRESS is a publisher of books, recordings, and DVDs on Christian spirituality. Our publishing represents a full expression of Christian belief and practice—from Catholic to Evangelical, from Protestant to Orthodox.

We are the publishing arm of the Community of Jesus, an ecumenical monastic community in the Benedictine tradition. As such, we are uniquely positioned in the marketplace without connection to a large corporation and with informal relationships to many branches and denominations of faith.

What We Are Doing

BOOKS | Paraclete publishes books that show the richness and depth of what it means to be Christian. Although Benedictine spirituality is at the heart of all that we do, we publish books that reflect the Christian experience across many cultures, time periods, and houses of worship. We publish books that nourish the vibrant life of the church and its people—books about spiritual practice, formation, history, ideas, and customs.

We have several different series, including the best-selling Living Library, Paraclete Essentials, and Paraclete Giants series of classic texts in contemporary English; A Voice from the Monastery—men and women monastics writing about living a spiritual life today; award-winning literary faith fiction and poetry; and the Active Prayer Series that brings creativity and liveliness to any life of prayer.

RECORDINGS | From Gregorian chant to contemporary American choral works, our music recordings celebrate sacred choral music through the centuries. Paraclete distributes the recordings of the internationally acclaimed choir Gloriæ Dei Cantores, praised for their "rapt and fathomless spiritual intensity" by *American Record Guide,* and the Gloriæ Dei Cantores Schola, which specializes in the study and performance of Gregorian chant. Paraclete is also the exclusive North American distributor of the recordings of the Monastic Choir of St. Peter's Abbey in Solesmes, France, long considered to be a leading authority on Gregorian chant.

DVDs | Our DVDs offer spiritual help, healing, and biblical guidance for life issues: grief and loss, marriage, forgiveness, anger management, facing death, and spiritual formation.

Learn more about us at our Web site:
www.paracletepress.com,
or call us toll-free at 1-800-451-5006.